Bucks County Ghost Stories

by

Charles J. Adams III

EXETER HOUSE BOOKS

1999

BUCKS COUNTY GHOST STORIES

©1999 Charles J. Adams III

Published by EXETER HOUSE BOOKS

All rights reserved under the copyright laws of the United States. With the exception of brief passages for review purposes, no portion of this book may be reproduced in print, electronically, or commercially without written permission from
EXETER HOUSE BOOKS,
P.O. Box 8134,
Reading, PA 19603

ISBN: 1-880683-13-X

FIRST EDITION JUNE 1999
PRINTED IN THE UNITED STATES OF AMERICA

BUCKS COUNTY GHOST STORIES
TABLE OF CONTENTS

·BUCKS COUNTY GHOST STORIES·

INTRODUCTION

And About the Authors

Before we begin our journey to the "other side" of life in Bucks County, allow me to introduce myself. Or, more properly, ourselves.

And let me also thank you for choosing to add this volume to your bookshelf.

This book was inevitable.

It had to happen.

After compiling chronicles of ghosts and legends in such diverse places as the concrete canyons of midtown Manhattan and the sandy dunes of Delaware; after researching and writing books on the supernatural from the Ohio to the Hudson, the Poconos to the Pine Barrens; this book had to happen.

For those not familiar with the kind of work my research and marketing partner David J. Seibold and I have carried out since the early 1980s, and who we are, I will explain.

David is a native of Willow Grove, Pennsylvania, but for most of his adult life has resided near Reading and has been employed as a senior account executive at radio station WEEU there.

He also maintains a residence in Barnegat Light, N.J., where he has volunteered with the resort town's rescue squad and has earned his commercial sea captain's license.

Through his passion for deep sea fishing and scuba diving, Dave collected detailed information about shipwrecks off the New Jersey coast and maintained a large file on each wreck.

As promotions director and morning air personality at WEEU radio, I had worked with Dave for several years before realizing that we had much in common–as well as many differences–all of which would serve each other well.

Dave and I shared an interest in the lore of the sea. Dave's interest stemmed from the way shipwrecks enhanced his fishing and diving exploits. Mine was more rooted in the human drama that played out in even the most pedantic maritime disaster.

I had already self-published and self-promoted three books about ghost stories and legends in my native Berks County. Each was embraced enthusiastically by a niche audience of readers.

Publication of those books was an extension of my early 1970s job as a writer for a newspaper in Reading (I am still a travel writer and columnist for the *Reading Eagle*) and my appreciation of regional history, legends, and folklore.

That appreciation led me to become involved as a director of the Historical Society of Berks County, trustee and then president of the Reading Public Library, and most recently a charter trustee of a library which was being established in my home of Exeter Township, Berks County, as this book was being written.

While I could express myself with some clarity in print, I fell pitifully short as a seller and promoter of my own words.

Somehow, in some fortuitous way, my and Dave's singular skills converged to form what we came to call Exeter House Books.

Our first publication as a team was, appropriately, *Shipwrecks Off Barnegat Inlet*.

From my meager beginnings peddling books out of car trunks and onto consignment ledgers to worldwide sales in major book store chains, catalogs, and the internet, our little collaboration–still, incidentally, more fun than work–has given us great satisfaction.

Our simple stories have been spun off into walking tours of haunted towns and cities, motorcoach tours at Halloween, various websites, television adaptations, and international ghost tours.

I truly hope that those of you who have purchased any of our books have found our work to be worth your time and money.

Our writing and publishing process has been almost frightfully simple. We research endearing and enduring ghost stories and legends in a particular place and lay a foundation upon which we build a book.

We plod through dusty documents, historical societies and museums; we probe newspaper morgues, spend countless hours on the internet, and then spend months wandering streets or roads to keep appointments with those who have stories to share.

Not until miles of tape and stacks of papers are accumulated do I sit before the iMac and put into print what had been scattered images, tattered notes, and stacks of interviews.

When my writing job is completed, Dave's marketing job begins.

For this volume, Dave and I were aided by and are forever indebted to Bucks County educator Monica Hartzel, who from her Doylestown home directed many of our efforts.

A longtime companion of Dave's, "Nicki" plunged into the project with an energy that reflected her pride in her native county and her vast knowledge and understanding of its people, places, and heritage.

Her father's family once owned a feed mill in Chalfont. Her mother's family once operated the Ottsville Inn. Nicki Hartzel is *real* Bucks County.

Bucks County is the tenth region Dave and I have chosen to examine and write about. And what, some may argue, qualifies us "outsiders" as keepers of the supernatural flame in this place? This place which nurtured and nurtures so many of its own fine writers?

It is the same creative spark that fired James Michener to set his sights far beyond the borders of his beloved Bucks County and write of adventures in the South Pacific, the Caribbean, Texas, and dozens of other places.

It is the same urge that prompted adopted Bucks Countian Oscar Hammerstein II to toil in his Bucks County retreat and tell magical stories about folks on an Oklahoma plain and an Austrian platz.

And, it is the desire that keeps a large community of contemporary Bucks County writers laboring in vain or fame.

I, too, crawl from a wellspring of writers in my own beloved *Berks* County, where the likes of Wallace Stevens (by day an insurance executive, by dreams a Pulitzer Prize-winning romantic poet) and John Updike grew from mere minnows into big fish of the literary lake.

I do not pretend to be in the company of these people. I can only hope to add a few more words, thoughts, and images to a few more pages.

I tell stories. That's all. In the vast estate of life and literature, I huddle by a campfire over in the corner, waiting for anyone who is curious to come and call.

You have ventured to that campfire. Gather around now and listen as I tell you stories of Bucks County....the *ghost stories* of Bucks County.

THE HAUNTED HOUSE ON HOLLY HILL

Mary, the Ghost of Bolton Mansion

The Bolton Mansion, Levittown

The Bolton Mansion stands out on a hill above the streets and houses of Levittown. And, it stands out as a triumph of perseverance by those who believe that history and heritage matter.

To be sure, Levittown has a history–a history which is very much a part of America's history in the second half of the 20th century.

That history should be noted, as it is also very much a part of the past, present, and future of Bolton Mansion–which, as you will soon discover–is the seat of some of the strongest supernatural energy in all of Bucks County.

As the salvation and preservation of the mansion is a study in appreciation of those who came before us, the development of Levittown is a study in a sociological phenomenon.

First, there is no Levittown, as such. What came to be called Levittown is similar to what came to be called Hershey. Pennsylvania's "Chocolate Town" exists only in name, and is in fact an unincorporated settlement inside Derry Township, Dauphin County. What was built as the second (the first was in 1947 on Long Island, N.Y.) Levittown was never incorporated and now spreads out in Bristol, Falls, and Middletown townships and Tullytown borough.

From 1952 to 1958, William J. Levitt's construction company built 17,311 homes on 17,311 70-by-100 foot lots. Each had one fruit tree, two willows, and 27 shrubs. Each had everything the others had. There were six models, eight colors, and a price range from $10,999 to $16,999. The basic model cost the buyer a $61 per month mortgage.

The streets were winding, every one of them, to keep cars from speeding through. The street names were alphabetized.

There were rules. Many rules. No fences. No parking on the street. No hanging of laundry on Sundays. No black people.

"That's right," an 86-year old William Levitt (whose family started building "affordable" housing around the U.S. Navy base in Norfolk, Virginia, in 1929) told Hofstra University professor Stuart Bird in 1986, "originally we would not sell to a black person because it was an old story that if we sold to blacks, whites would not buy." But Levitt met with black leaders and the color barrier for buyers broke in 1957. Other walls soon tumbled, as well.

What were described as "cookie-cutter" houses and by folk singer Pete Seeger as "little boxes made of ticky-tack" have since taken on diverse personalities.

As the community and the larger region around it has changed (Levitt targeted the former farmland for his development when U.S. Steel opened its Fairless plant), so has Levittown.

But through it all, in one corner of Levittown–Holly

Hill, and on Holly Drive–the Bolton Mansion held its own.

Also known as the Pemberton-Morris House, the mansion's oldest section dates to 1687, when Phineas Pemberton built it as the centerpiece of the 350-acre Bolton Farm, which he named after his wife's, Phoebe's, home in Lancashire, England.

Pemberton, considered by some to be the "father of Bucks County," was a confidante of William Penn (who called his friend "the ablest man in the province"), and held many positions in the early Provincial Government.

His great granddaughter Mary married Anthony Morris in 1790, and Morris added to Pemberton's original structure with what is now the "West Wing" of the home. With that, which expanded the building to 22 rooms, Bolton truly became a mansion.

Morris was President Madison's ambassador to Spain and the man who negotiated the purchase of Florida from that country. His family continued to own the property through its occupancy by Effingham Morris, a civic leader, officer of the Pennsylvania Railroad, and president of the former Girard Bank.

After his death, the family turned the farm over to the University of Pennsylvania, which operated its veterinary sciences school there.

The property later became an executive mansion for U.S. Steel and then the property of William Levitt, who pared the original estate to six acres. But, at least, the mansion was not demolished in favor of a few more 70x100 foot lots.

Later, it became the Bristol Township municipal building and police station.

When the township moved to larger quarters in 1966, the glory years of Bolton Mansion were left in its wake.

Throughout the late 1960s, vandals and vagrants made the mansion their home and the once-stately building where Revolutionary War officers once dined became a dangerous derelict.

Several attempts were made to save the mansion, but not until the Friends of Bolton Mansion, Inc. was formed and an alliance with the Bucks County Conservancy was forged was the stabilization and restoration of Bolton Mansion assured.

"On the evening the contract for demolition was to be awarded, we were at the meeting," said Jim Snow, one of the founders of the Friends.

"A firm was awarded the bid. But on that same evening a courier came up front of the township meeting and delivered a letter from Governor Milton Shapp urging that they not tear the building down until the state could send a representative to meet with the township to find a way to save the building."

After inching onto the on-ramp to rehabilitation, the

citizens group turned into the acceleration lane.

"We had no expertise," Snow continued. "We just had a love of history and of this building. We knew that if it was ever torn down, it could never be recreated."

The conservancy took over the deed to the property, and the restoration was up to full speed.

Since then, the Friends got the deed back, and with a large and energetic core of volunteers, the project has proceeded swiftly.

Hopefully by the time you read this, Bolton Mansion is up and running in full restoration.

Such was not the case upon the occasion of our visit in late winter, 1999.

Those volunteers were abuzz with activities in the house and nearby tenants' quarters. The interior had been stripped to its oldest and strongest beams. There were tangles of new wiring, old wiring. Walls were virtually non-existent within the shell of the structure.

What was once a grand staircase in the front of the mansion was obscured somewhere within the orderly chaos.

And somewhere, invisible to all who put their time and toil into the restoration effort, was the resident ghost of Bolton Mansion.

Or, more properly, the resident *ghosts* of the house on Holly Hill.

Just about everybody who has anything to do with

Bolton Mansion has heard of its unseen tenants. Jim Snow certainly has.

"I'm not sure if it was a servant girl or a member of the family," he reported, "but she hung herself in the mansion.

"Her name was Mary. It seems that she was going with a soldier and, as close as we can determine, it was back during the Civil War era.

"She wasn't permitted to see her friend anymore, so she hung herself here," he pointed, "on the front staircase."

The enlightened administration of the Friends of Bolton Mansion learned early on that Mary, or better yet Mary's *ghost* could actually play a major role in the funding of the renovations of the big house.

"When we got started with this project back in the '70s," Snow recalled, "we operated a haunted house here."

It was a typical Halloween season walk-through-get-scared-by-creepy-creatures "Haunted House," put on originally for the benefit of the local Easter Seals chapter, and then the township recreation center, and finally for the benefit of the Friends.

In autumn, around Halloween, the moon rises over the rear of the property, giving it the perfect "high and windy hill" atmosphere for a good, scare 'em up "haunted" attraction.

Thing is...the place is really haunted!

Tens of thousands of folks streamed through its doors as the old house became one of the premier seasonal attractions in lower Bucks County.

At the end of one of the years of operation, the Friends held a "thank you" party for its volunteers. They offered the volunteers–mostly teenagers–two options for entertainment: (A) A rock band, or (B) Some professor who would tell them about his findings regarding paranormal activities in the Bolton Mansion.

The teens overwhelmingly rejected the rock for the prof.

Coming from the scientific end of such research, the professor (actually a student of the paranormal) took several infrared photographs in the mansion under strictly controlled conditions.

In the Winter, 1977, *Journal of Occult Studies*, Donald Gibson, Jr., revealed his findings in the photographic experiment which was sanctioned by Bucks County Community College.

With a team of volunteers from the college, and with the full cooperation of the township police, the project was undertaken, but little was determined.

Bluish/greenish glows made barely discernible shapes on the resulting photographs, and Gibson said the face of an "old hag or gargoyle" could be seen in one of them.

Jim Snow remembered the occasion, and that while 95 percent of the pictures were inconclusive, at best, two did stand out.

"One of them showed what could be a hoop skirt in the bottom portion of the picture. The other showed what you could say was the side profile of a man with a stripe going down the center of his pants leg."

With a little imagination, one could say that the hoop skirt image could have been Mary and the stripe could have been on the uniform of her ill-fated lover.

Some volunteers claim to have actually seen a faint, misty figure ascend the front staircase. Others say they've heard what they described as muffled moans and stifled screams at the bottom and top of those stairs.

And, the ghostly activities at Bolton Mansion aren't limited to within the walls of the mansion.

It is said a woman's ghost has been spotted rambling between the tenants' house in the rear of the property to the east side of the mansion. It appears to be rushing back and forth, as if searching for something or someone.

And, at least one neighbor told us that she had often seen a glowing form gliding across the front yard of the house.

The woman, who asked we not use her name, said that on one occasion she witnessed that form gliding toward the house, disappearing into a wall, and reappearing as a glowing face, gazing from the second floor, front window of the oldest section of the house.

In the summer of 1998, more than two dozen members of the Philadelphia Ghost Hunters Alliance were accompanied by Jim Snow on nearly three-hour investigation of paranormal activities in and around the Bolton Mansion.

The investigators were equipped with thermal scanners, night vision scopes with infrared illuminators, and other equipment which can detect aberrations in light, sound, and temperature.

Lewis Gerew, president of the PGHA, filed a detailed report on his experiences.

Almost as soon as Gerew flicked on the switch of his night vision scope, something unsettling happened:

To my amazement, I got some results I didn't know were possible. With my night vision scope, I surprisingly saw what I perceived to be an ectoplasmic vapor. I could see it motionless, just outside a third floor window.

Even as I veered my scope to either side, trying to see if the lens was fogged or stained, the vapor remained stationary. I wiped my eyes in my disbelief and looked again. It was still there.

I reasoned that, had it been a low-lying cloud, it would have moved at least a little. Having witnessed this for a few minutes, I made not of it and moved on.

Making my way around the building with no

further results, I decided to pay the ecto one more visit before investigating inside the mansion. It was no longer there.

To satisfy my skepticism of a possible trick of lighting, I maneuvered my way around the area to try and duplicate what I saw initially through the scope. I was unsuccessful and accepted that what I saw was real.

Later, in a room to the rear of the house, Gerew and others in the group felt very uneasy and reported seeing what Gerew called "occasional wisps of movement coming from both sides of the room near the back wall."

As the party made its way past the front staircase and through rooms on all levels of the house, members said they felt as if they were being followed. Two reported what they could only describe as the sound of a little girl laughing.

"Chills were frequent for all of us and some could smell an unfamiliar odor," Gerew wrote. And, his report included descriptions of equipment quirks, a 55-gallon drum which seemingly moved on its own to block their progress at one point, and a conclusion that yes, Bolton Mansion is quite haunted.

"Never before," Gerew said on behalf of his fellow investigators, "have any of us experienced an event of this magnitude.

"Bizarre things were continually happening all

around us. The best I could do was soak in the experience and try to make sense of it all."

Does the notion of one, two, three, or however many ghosts inhabiting the Bolton Mansion deter its volunteers from doing their work? Not at all.

"After all the research that's been done," Jim Snow said, "it's been determined that our ghosts are friendly ghosts."

Indeed, nothing untoward has ever happened to anybody at Bolton Mansion during the restoration project or the PGHA investigation, and everyone seems quite comfortable with those who apparently are also comfortable enough about the place to stick around...for eternity.

•

Ancient graves believed to be those of Native Americans at a cemetery near Gallows Hill.

JACOB–IS THAT YOU, JACOB?

The Ghost of an Old Innkeeper Has Some Trembling in Trumbauersville

The Trum Tavern, Trumbauersville

The Trum Tavern has anchored the busy town of Trumbauersville since well before the American Revolution.

Of course, the tavern–and the town–would be barely recognizable to colonials these days.

The first drinks were served at what is now the Trum Tavern by Elisha Parker in 1752. Town meetings were held there, wayfarers found lodging there, and stage coaches stopped there.

It has a long and proud history, does that Trum Tavern.

And, it has a ghost.

If the suspicions of some of those who have met the presence are correct, that ghost is a rather noteworthy ghost.

In its position in extreme northeastern Bucks County, Trumbauersville is a bit off the beaten paths of the busy routes 309 and 663 which meet in nearby Quakertown.

Ever-encroaching "progress" is engulfing the area and much of what *was* has disappeared or is disappearing in tangles of traffic and commerce.

Still, there are many who treasure the history of the towns and townships of that corner of Bucks County. They fought to have Route 663 named the John Fries Highway as it courses through Milford Township, and encouraged developers to name streets for other important figures in what has gone down in history as the Fries Rebellion.

A footnote in the reams of Revolutionary War stories, the Fries Rebellion took root when barrel-maker and auctioneer John Fries incited residents of Milford Township to oppose a property tax (the "Direct Tax") which the federal government levied in 1798.

The tax receipts were supposedly to be used in anticipation of a war against France–a war which never happened.

Fries, from the pulpit of his auction podium, encouraged property owners in and around that part of Bucks County to reject the taxation. In 1799, Governor Thomas Mifflin ordered militia units from Reading and Bethlehem to march into the Quakertown area and subdue any resistors.

Fries amassed several dozen armed men in Quakertown and proceeded to lead them through a variety of actions of what some called "treason" and others may have called "civil disobedience."

Eventually, however, the government did call it treason, did try and convict John Fries, and sentenced him to be hanged.

Two days before the scheduled executions of Fries and several of his compatriots, President John Adams pardoned them. They were later praised as heroes both in Bucks County and in the annals of history.

Furthermore, the ramifications of the Fries Rebellion continue to be cited and debated in such contemporary matters of gun control and federal pardons.

As this book was being written, U.S. Supreme Court Chief Justice William Rehnquist, who had presided over the Senate impeachment trial of President William Clinton, reflected on past impeachments which included that of Supreme Court Associate Justice Samuel Chase.

Chief Justice Rehnquist stated that one of three bases of Chase's impeachment was his conduct in John Fries' trial and the death sentence he imposed on Fries. Rehnquist agreed that President Adams' pardon, against the unanimous advice from his cabinet, was to Adams' credit.

Very well. What does all this have to do with ghosts?

As it turns out, one of John Fries' relatives–it has never really been determined what, if any, the relationship was–may be around in ethereal form at the old Trum Tavern.

That's what Arlene De Vitis believes.

A fill-in cook and resident of the second floor of the tavern, Arlene is certain there is a spirit in the building, and is reasonably certain it is that of Jacob Fries.

Once the Jacob Fries Tavern, and in more recent

years simply "Jake's," what is now the Trum Tavern has long had a reputation as being haunted.

"I've lived in a haunted house before," Arlene said, "so I know what it's like."

She feels the overpowering sense that she's never alone up on that second floor. And yet, she's comfortable with that feeling.

Arlene said the presence actually follows her, sometimes even out of the tavern building and down the street. And, the ghost is not only felt, but seen and heard.

"It's an old man with gray hair," she recalled. "It's like you can see an outline. He's dressed in black. And occasionally I can hear him banging around upstairs."

Others who work, worked, live, or lived in the tavern building agree that there are many unexplainable noises, several incomprehensible sightings, and some unanswerable questions about the ancient place where Jacob, or whomever it may be, seems to have free reign.

Helen Huber, who was 79 years old at the time we spoke with her, had worked in the inn for 30 years and through a half-dozen innkeepers. She heard many strange sounds, and felt that same everpresent sensation that she was not alone. She agreed the tavern was haunted, and that the ghost was none other than Jacob Fries.

Down the street at a town deli, Sandy Snyder

recalled her time spent working as a bartender in the tavern.

"I worked there for three years," she said, "and would never want to be in there alone."

Sandy concurred with the others that Jacob's spirit was still in the tavern, and would at times make itself very well known.

"He would open the door into the beer room. I could actually see the door slowly open and close on its own," she said.

Another time, she and a former owner were closing up the building at night. All circuit breakers were shut off, but one–one which Sandy swore had no electrical service surging into it–flipped itself on. She, the owner, and one other individual who was with them at the time, fled in fear.

That other individual, incidentally, was the electrician!

Sandy remembered that it was Room 1 on the second floor in which she and others at the time believed the energy was strongest. And when Sandy said "strong," she meant it.

"Oh, yeah," she said, "it was strong. One time, I was downstairs and I swear, the ghost pushed me."

Other parts of the Trum Tavern where the energy seems to be strongest are on the existing stairs and an area where a staircase once stood.

There are some who question the existence of a ghost in the tavern, but for those who have encountered the sights and sounds in the building, there is no doubt.

As Sandy Snyder said unequivocally, "I know that place is haunted. I believe it in my heart."

•

THINGS THAT GO BUMP IN BUCKSVILLE

Seances, Guests Report Haunting of Bucksville House

The Bucksville House Bed & Breakfast, Kintnersville.

The Bucksville House, along Route 412, is a charming country inn close to Nockamixon State Park, New Hope, the river village of Kintnersville, and all that makes Bucks County, well, Bucks County.

But before we go any farther, let us be clear about the name of the *Bucks*ville House.

Bucks County, of course, received its name from Buckinghamshire, England. Bucksville received its name from Capt. Nicholas Buck, who established a working village on the Durham Road in 1795. Capt. Buck, who gathered area men and formed a militia during the Revolution, also fought in the War of 1812. It is believed he trained his militia troops in fields which surround the present inn.

By the early 1800s, Buck's residence became a stagecoach stop and tavern called "The White Horse." In about 1831, Buck's son, Nicholas Jr., expanded the building and operated it as the Bucksville Hotel.

It has stood for many more recent years as a bed and breakfast with cozy common rooms, five tasteful guest rooms, a gazebo, lovely grounds...and a good ghost story.

Barbara and Joe Szollosi, who have lived in the place since 1984, are quite at home with those ghosts, and their guests seem to have no trouble accepting them. In fact, several guests have willingly helped perpetuate the many tales of the unexplained that revolve around the Bucksville House.

The Szollosis, both former school teachers, lived there with their 21-pound cat, "Muffy," when we visited and asked about their very well-known hauntings. And, incidentally, we do not mention Muffy frivolously.

"People have told me that Muffy would know if there was an *evil* spirit here," said Barbara, "but she's very calm. So, we believe most of the spirits in the house are pretty nice."

Most? More than one ghost in the Bucksville House?

Keep reading.

According to research the Szollosis have done on their property, what they call the 1795 Room really dates back to that year, and was originally a wheelwright's shop. Its woodburning stove, Mercer tile floor, and rustic beauty is a showpiece of the inn. And, it may well be the epicenter of energy in the Bucksville House.

"We had a seance here in April, 1998, in this room," Barbara continued. She added that the findings of the seance were startling.

"We sat around the table. They brought in a lot of paraphernalia. They brought in a pyramid, black candles, crystals, sage, holy water, salt water, a cross–it took them a half-hour just to set up!.

"Through a 'caller,' who chanted, three spirits entered the room."

Barbara was told to speak, through the "caller," to the assembled entities. She told she welcomed them to her home.

Through the mediums, it was determined that there was strong energy in the yard. The energy predated the house. And, it was probably related to hostilities between the natives and earliest settlers.

Then again, as we mentioned earlier, it is generally accepted that in that yard Capt. Buck drilled his citizen soldiers. Perhaps it their energy that remains in the field.

But it is not only on the grounds around the inn where spirit activity has been detected.

A strong presence has also been confirmed in at least one of the guest rooms upstairs. Barbara and Joe have confirmed it, visiting psychics and mediums have confirmed it–but more significantly, guests have confirmed it.

"We have had guests stay here who said they have experienced people here, as well as noises, things moving, etc.," Barbara continued.

"The strongest energy is the ghost of a man who paces between the fireplace and the window. He's very agitated, very unsettled. He keeps coming over to the bed, and in the bed is his son, who is not well."

Barbara even "tested" the energy with the aid of a divining rod. Previous readings were substantiated when the rods abruptly split as to indicate energy at spots in the inn which were previously "read" psychically.

There are marked "cold spots" throughout the inn, and several items have been lost–and then found in the most unexpected places. Maids have reported conversations coming from empty rooms, soft touches on their shoulders, and shadowy forms drifting through the rooms. Disembodied footsteps–sometimes very pronounced footsteps on the tile floors–have been and still are common. The Szollosis even have several photographs which were taken during their renovations and contain anomalies which are difficult to explain and, Barbara believes, may be actual pictures of their otherwise invisible inhabitants.

Barbara said one of the most interesting encounters they've ever had was when the former owners of the house dropped by just after the Szollosis had completed their renovations and fired a broadside at the new innkeepers.

"They asked us if we had any experiences yet with the ghost," Barbara said. "They told us their son had reported a man standing at the foot of his bed many, many times.

"The boy wasn't scared, and told his parents the man had a flat black hat and a string tie. He just stood there and watched him."

Again, in no case was any harm done to anyone by the spirits of the Bucksville House.

Over the years, the house has picked up a reputation in that part of Bucks County as being haunted, and the owners are quite at home with that.

The ghosts of the Bucksville House have been heard, seen, and felt by many. Although regarded as quite benign, the energies there did frighten one cleaning lady who, when vacuuming, said she heard a phantom voice instructing, "Turn it off...turn it off now!"

Seeing no one near her, and knowing she was alone, she calmly did turn the vacuum off and fled, never to venture upstairs alone again.

In one room on the second floor, in the oldest part the house, a weak spirit has been discovered. It's believed to be that of a woman who died in that room during childbirth.

On the third floor, an attic where drovers were once given cheap accommodations, a young boy's ghost holds fort. Quite playful, the boy's spirit has toyed with guests, and Joe Szollosi thinks he's even followed him downstairs where he teases Joe in his workshop.

Again, it is the feedback from guests at the Bucksville House which reveal the most intriguing stories.

"We don't tell people about our unseen guests at first," Barbara noted. But, on the very morning of our interview with Mrs. Szollosi in January, 1999, another guest checked out with another paragraph for this story.

"A woman came down for breakfast today and asked us if we had any spirits. We asked her why, and she said she saw someone standing at the foot of the bed. She could see his outline, and watched it disappear. She was amazed!"

Without a doubt, the most telling of all feedback the Szollosis have received regarding their ghosts came from a Riverton, N.J., woman who had been a guest there in 1993.

In a letter the innkeepers cherish, the writer gave a stirring account of her night at the Bucksville House:

While reading in the sitting room of the suite upstairs, I suddenly had the feeling I was not alone.

I looked all around the room and knew that she was there. I didn't actually see her–not clearly anyway–but I knew she was dressed in off-white with soft pleats on the bodice and skirt and wearing a soft nightcap. She was quite rotund with clinched-in waist below a large bosom. She was smiling and seemed slightly retarded or perhaps just not very bright.

She liked my being there in her room–I felt accepted. She looked more like a peasant than a lady.

The surprising thing was that I was not at all alarmed or frightened. In fact, it was comforting to have her there. Almost all night I would turn off the light, try to sleep, turn it on again and read, turned off the light, tried to sleep, etc. She stayed all night.

The guest added that she also felt the presence "on and off" in the dining room of the inn.

And despite her adventure that nearly sleepless night, the writer added an interesting postscript:

Thanks for a terrific weekend. We enjoyed Bucksville House so much. Your quilts, decor, and breakfasts are fantastic. Hopefully, we'll be back!

We add our own postscript to the story. Not an hour before our visit to the Bucksville House, Barbara had placed a foot stool at a particular place in a particular room on the second floor. As we wound our way through the rooms of this most charming inn, we came into that room, Barbara stopped dead in her tracks.

"Oh, dear," she exclaimed, "this is giving me the chills! That chair has moved."

And so it had. Barbara swore that the foot stool had moved some five feet from where she knew she had placed it earlier.

Enter, once more, the research team from the Philadelphia Ghost Hunters Alliance.

Alliance president Lewis Gerew and seven others were given a tour of the house by Barbara Szollosi, and the investigators came across several suspected "hot spots" of spectral activity. Gerew had one particular experience which peaked his curiosity:

As I made my way across the sitting room I heard what sounded like two glasses clanging behind me. I stopped and quickly turned around. The noise stopped just as fast as I turned.

However, when I did look behind me, I searched for an explanation of the sound. The only thing that came to mind (that could have caused that noise) was the glass chandelier hanging above me and about five feet behind me.

Although the chandelier was completely still, I immediately assumed that my weight on the old wood floors caused the chandelier to shake and cause the sound.

I did try to recreate the sound by walking back and forth across the room. Each time I was unsuccessful.

I never heard the sound again.

It is interesting to note at this point that the Bucksville House is one of several bed and breakfasts and inns throughout Bucks County that willingly told their ghost stories for publication.

There were others with ghost stories–in some cases very good ghost stories–but they declined to allow publication of the stories for fear that the notion of a ghost in a guest room might chase away prospective customers.

Our first experience with this reluctance to publicize ghostly occurrences in inns or B&Bs was in charming, Victorian Cape May.

As we researched our first book in that New Jersey

resort city, we scoured the streets and stopped at virtually every inn in town.

For simplicity, let us say 50 of those inns confirmed there were ghost stories connected to them. Of that 50, however, let's say only 25 allowed us to publish the stories. The other 25 believed that if folks knew their place was "haunted," they'd decide against staying there.

When the first book hit the shelves, those other 25 stories were included. And when, say, fifteen of the inns that refused to be in the book noticed that many people actually *wanted* to stay in the other inns because they *did* have a ghost story, they wondered why we didn't use their stories.

Whether a haunting is good or bad for business is the decision of the business owner. But we feel, and experience has supported it, that a good ghost story gives a place–be it a B&B, restaurant, house, town, or county–character.

In none of the hundreds of ghost stories we have investigated have "evil" spirits infected a place and turned it into a chamber of horrors.

There certainly have been frightening experiences that have caught people off guard, but no actual harm has come to anyone we have ever interviewed.

Franklin D. Roosevelt summed it up when he said, "The only thing we have to fear...is fear itself."

•

THE WATCHER OF THE WATERS

The Guardian Ghost of Lake Nockamixon

The Blue Heron Inn, Nockamixon State Park

At the southernmost corner of Lake Nockamixon, where Three Mile Run and Tohickon Creek meet, is a remarkable reminder of another era in this section of Bucks County where a state park has forever changed the landscape.

As much as the eight-mile long, 1,500-acre manmade lake and the 5,000-acre park which surrounds it has indeed altered the land, all those changes have not suppressed the legend of "The Watcher of the Waters."

One of the few reminders of the area before the state park was built in the 1960s is The Blue Heron Inn on Lake Nockamixon.

Older Bucks Countians may know the elegant lakeside inn as The Lake House Inn. For more than two decades, the DuBree family operated the restaurant under that name. In the late 1990s, Janet Healy purchased the place and gave it the new name.

And, another generation of Bucks Countians would remember a time when the inn was *not* lakeside at all.

According to Ms. Healy, the inn can be traced to the early 19th century when it was the Church Hill General Store. Along with the store, a creamery, grist mill, and livery stable were situated nearby. It served as a stop for the stagecoaches that rolled between Bethlehem and Philadelphia.

In the 1860s, the Weisel family bought the store, established a post office, and gave the little community their name.

"The general store also served as a gathering spot for local folks," Ms. Healy noted. "Domino games were a weekly occurrence and sleds would be seen lined up outside while hot chocolate and apple cider was served to all."

A fire destroyed a portion of the store in 1965, and when it was determined that the building would be spared from the flooding needed to form the lake, it was decided that the structure be saved, rebuilt, and named The Lake House Inn.

Now the Blue Heron Inn, it is positioned above the lake and affords diners a lovely view and elegant dining.

And for those patrons with a sense of adventure, the Blue Heron also provides an interesting story.

Janet Healy provided the details:

"On the south shore of Lake Nockamixon, near The Blue Heron, there have been sightings and stories about the lone man on the lake in an ancient canoe.

"Long before the lake was created, the area was inhabited by the Lenape Indians. The three natural creeks that now feed into the lake were utilized by this tribe for fishing and canoeing.

"When the Army Engineers went about creating the lake, they had no idea there was an Indian burial ground within the plain they would flood.

"This 'Happy Hunting Ground' was flooded, along

with several houses, barns, and a church to create Lake Nockamixon.

"According to Indian tradition, this was a violation to those who were put to rest there.

"The area now has numerous stories about that lone man in a canoe who travels the waters of the lake. Those who have seen him at a distance claim he is a native Indian in typical Indian dress.

"The canoe with its lone passenger has been spotted only when there is a mist or fog over the lake and the canoe disappears mysteriously into that haze.

"It is said that Indian tradition dictates that when their burial grounds are disturbed in any way it must be protected by the spirit of the tribe.

"'The Watcher of the Waters,' which is what he has been named, silently slips on the surface of Lake Nockamixon–and on especially quiet nights the rapping of drums permeates the air over the water as if to signal that this phantom still continues to watch over those who rest below."

•

Haycock Mountain looms beyond the waters of Lake Nockamixon.

·BUCKS COUNTY GHOST STORIES·

A MOUNTAIN CALLED "GHOST" AND A LANE CALLED "HAUNTED"

Many Bucks Place Names Have Bizarre Origins

The road to Ghost Mountain.

·BUCKS COUNTY GHOST STORIES·

No compilation of ghost stories and legends of Bucks County would be complete without mention of some of the county's most bizarre people and places.

While many people venture no farther into Bucks County than New Hope, Lahaska, or the malls and recreation centers; there is a deep, proud, and sometimes very strange history to this place.

This is a place with a public lane called *Haunted* Lane. It is a place with a Gallows Hill, a Devil's Hole, a Devil's Half-Acre, a ravine named Outlaw Pass, a rock formation called Dragon's Mouth, and a hill called Ghost Mountain.

And although a certain level of sophistication has altered the way of life here, Bucks County still retains many reminders of its strong Pennsylvania German heritage–complete with ancient superstitions stories that date to its earliest settlers.

Ghost Mountain

We will begin this chapter with a visit to a ridge close to Springtown near Bucks' northern border.

It is a ridge that rises some 650 feet and is officially named Cressman Hill.

But for generations of folks who have lived in that bucolic section of the county, that ridge is Ghost Mountain.

While the more practical sorts who live in the area reject any notion of ghosts on Ghost Mountain, there are others who reach back into time-worn tales and retain the folklore that has wrapped around the ridge since at least the early part of the 20th century.

In 1990, the Springfield Township Historical Society solicited and later published several accounts from township residents who shared their recollections of how and why Ghost Mountain became known as such.

In an odd juxtaposition of nomenclature, the closest village to Ghost Mountain is Pleasant Valley. Marvin Kunsman, of that village, offered his explanation. "Go over the bridge at Cook's Creek," he said, "and go straight up Ghost Mountain hill. At certain times mist and fog starts. The wind whistles and howls through the trees. The mist and fog come down over the woods and rises up from the ground and it looks like ghosts. That's how it got its name."

Another lifelong resident of the township blamed the name on an old man with a white beard who used to don a white sheet at night and run through the woods scaring children from his property.

Still another individual remembered that they were told that a woman hanged herself in a small shack near the base of Ghost Mountain and that incident spawned the legend and name.

As we looked for any signs of ghosts on Ghost Mountain, we heard more stories. Christine Lanning, who took time out from her work as a local paramedic, said she remembered stories about a man being murdered on top of the mountain and his headless ghost roaming the ridge.

Robert Zisco heard a similar story, but of a man who became disoriented and lost in the woods on the hillside. He was never found, and it's presumed his remains are still up there somewhere–as is his aimless spirit.

And Grace Strawn Bleam, who lived on top of Ghost Mountain when she was a ten-year old in 1922. "It was called Strawn's Point," she recalled, "because my grandfather, Mahlon Strawn, bought the house and lived there. The Cressman Mill was right below the hill. Mr. Clinton Daniels lived catty-cornered down the street. He had a lot of kids. They believed in hexoria and pow-wow. They believed in ghosts. They were spooky and they called it Ghost Mountain."

One man who owns property and lives on the side of Ghost Mountain admitted he has heard all the stories, but pooh-poohs any possibility of any ghosts.

"The legend is relatively recent and largely inaccurate and for me is, frankly, a pain in the butt." He says the old tales still draw the occasional "ghost hunters" who pass by and bother the handful of residents in the area.

Indeed, that area is strewn with rumors, myths, and superstitions. There are countless references to pyramids, cults, vortices, carcasses, sacrifices, altars, treasures, and, of course, ghosts in that rural section of the county.

Much of all of that could well be inventions, extensions, exaggerations, and enhancements of ancient folk tales. After all, not far north is *Hexenkopf*, a rocky outcropping in Northampton County where the early German settlers believed witches dwelled; and not far west is *Hexe Baerrick*, or "Witches' Hill," thought by early Berks Countians to be the home of witches.

So, like it or not–*truly* haunted or not–those people at that place called Ghost Mountain are merely caught in a web of legend that will cling forever to the dark corners of the archives of Bucks County history into which some people prefer not to tread.

Devil's Half Acre

Crammed between canal, river and road, a chunk of Bucks County land has been forever stained with a name which is apparently the legacy of bawdy, raucous times along the old canal.

If you blink, you'll miss "Devil's Half Acre" as you drive along Route 32 near Uhlerstown. And, while there seems to be little evidence of any actual hauntings in any of the handful of homes in the "half acre," there is an interesting origin of the unusual name.

Actually, the Prince of Darkness has somehow left his mark in several places throughout Bucks County–if in name only.

Up river from Devil's Half Acre is the Durham Cave, which was known locally as "Devil's Hole" because of the belief by some that anything bad that took place in that area of the county was the result of the evil spirits that dwelled inside the legendary, bat-infested cave.

Downstream is the natural rock formation called the "Devil's Tea Table."

As for Devil's Half Acre, some say it was given that name in the 19th century by a preacher who bore witness to the debauchery and sin which played out in a canal-side tavern near there. The drinking, the gambling, the harlotry–all, he claimed, were the work of the Devil on that half-acre along the waterway.

Dark Hollow

Dark Hollow Road in Warwick Township is severed by a broken-down bridge over the Neshaminy Creek. Along its course south from Swamp Road and north from Almshouse Road, the narrow macadam lane is lined with new homes and old homesteads.

And, where an old schoolhouse once stood, a ghost still dwells.

It is the ghost, local legend maintains, of a cruel early 19th century schoolmaster who beat and bethwacked his pupil so savagely that he was literally chased away from the old school by enraged parents.

The schoolmaster fled to parts unknown, never to

return to the old school house–never, that is, in human form.

The school building was vacated after the teacher was fired, and it soon fell into ruin.

One early evening, a former student of the old schoolmaster happened past the little building.

His attention was drawn to the schoolhouse by the sound of a banging shutter.

He ventured toward the school and decided to take a peek into the darkened, deserted room in which the tyrannical teacher once ruled with an iron switch.

To his shock and horror, the young man saw, standing inside the classroom, the faintly glowing figure of the old schoolmaster. The ghost had a thick tree branch in one hand, and seemed to be staring at the door of the schoolhouse as if to be waiting for another victim to enter.

Several folks who now live along Dark Hollow Road told us that they have heard the tale, and some said they believe they have seen the schoolmaster's spirit prowling along the side of the old road.

Gallows Hill

Not far south from Devil's Half Acre is Marshall Island, where tradition has it the ghost of Elizabeth Marshall maintains an eternal vigil.

Some accounts report the forlorn spirit along the towpath of the canal, others have seen her misty, glowing form on the island itself.

Elizabeth, who was pregnant, was murdered by Indians in 1755 in the Marshall home farther up the river. After the attack on his home, Edward Marshall moved what was left of his family to the island opposite Tinicum.

Edward Marshall's name is commemorated in the island's name to this day because Edward Marshall is important to Bucks County–and American–history.

Marshall was a walker in the infamous "Walking Purchase," which stepped off at 6 a.m., September 19, 1737, from a point near the Wrightstown Meeting House.

It was an event which cheated the natives of much land and which was a spark which helped to kindle the French and Indian War.

For his labors, Edward Marshall was promised land by the Penn family. He, too, was cheated by the provincial government and, at the same time, hated by the Indians. Hence the attack on his home and the killing of his wife.

Which leads us to Gallows Hill.

Old documents mention the tiny village of Gallows, which, in the late 19th century, had a post office, a tavern, and a few houses.

Near Gallows was Gallows Hill and Gallows Run.

And how did the village, the hill, and the creek get

their rather unpleasant names?

In an 1888 submission to the Buckwampun Historical Society, Jordan F. Stover wrote:

"Tradition tells us that the name 'Gallows Hill' was applied in consequence of an unknown traveler having

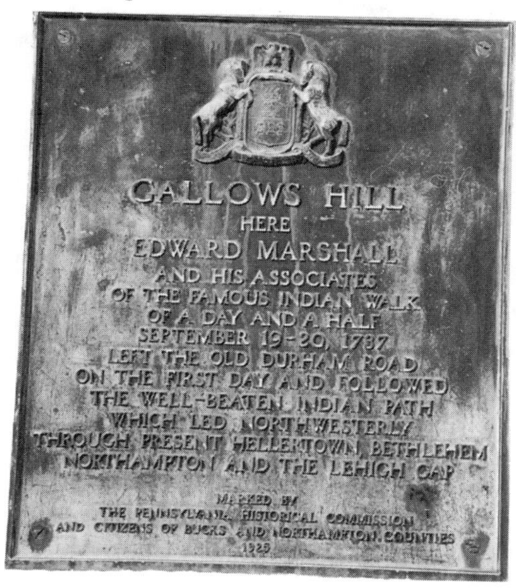

been found suspended by a rope attached to a limb of a chestnut tree by the roadside, who had committed suicide."

But another account, undated and unattributed, offers another explanation.

"A more amusing story of the origin of the name," the writer stated, "seems quite current in this locality to the effect that Edward Marshall, the walker, broke his *gallowses* (an archaic word for suspenders) in jumping across the run and, substituting some other support for his garments left the gallowses hanging on a tree at the brookside."

Haunted Lane

Let us travel nearly the entire length of Bucks County to Bensalem and visit yet another oddity, a roadway by the name of "Haunted Lane."

The lane links State Road and the Bristol Pike (Route 13) and curves with the bends of the Neshaminy Creek.

Several tidy homes and creekside cottages share Haunted Lane with modern industrial and warehouse buildings. And all share the unusual address.

The name is traced to the old Palthorpe Mansion which once stood along the road and what was once Lake Louise. As the old place deteriorated in time, it took on the appearance and reputation of being the local "haunted house."

One resident of Haunted Lane, Fred Wohlgemuth, said the "hauntings" were further fueled by the antics of men who'd gather in the house for some clandestine and high-stakes poker games.

Ed Brodecki, whose boat yard at 900 Haunted Lane has been in his family since 1952, told us he heard the same stories, and said the mysterious rattling chains and spine-chilling sounds that came from the old "haunted house" were really noises made by a lookout to scare away anybody who ventured near the house when the gambling was underway.

Whatever, as more and more summer homes were built in what became known as "Bridgewater," the old lane became known as Haunted Lane.

As the area became more gentrified in the 1950s, so did the name of the road. It became "Totem Road."

But, in 1976, the name of the winding way was restored to its original, ominous appellation.

Ringing Rocks

Just west of Upper Black Eddy is a Bucks County Park named after the four-acre sea of boulders, many of which, when struck with a hammer, will ring with metallic resonance. They say the ringing is the result of an unusually high crystal content in the rocks, which are said to be some ten feet deep at times.

And while we cannot offer up any ghost stories in or around Ringing Rocks Park, we can tell you there is

Ringing Rocks Park.

at least one individual who read much more into the resonance of Ringing Rocks.

The rocks have been investigated by a Maryland-based paranormal research team called "The Enigma Project," and by anomalist Ivan T. Sanderson who, in his book *Things*, said of Ringing Rocks, "something is frightfully wrong here."

Hermits, Pirates, Wizards and Witches

If the some of the *places* of Bucks County provide good copy, some of the *people* in the county's past are also worth noting.

Consider folks like Crazy Tom, and Bert the Hermit.

Crazy Tom

Thomas Meredith was believed to have been an educated, well-traveled young man who was left in the care of his cousin after his father died, sometime in the mid 1700s.

His father's passing had left Thomas despondent and confused. He wandered the family's sprawling farm and met an old Indian woman with whom he carried on one-way conversations.

He told anyone who would listen that the old woman was really a beautiful young woman, but her beauty would only emerge after he built a round castle tower. He said he learned this through a vision of someone he called "Melvin the Great Enchanter."

Tom–who came to be known as Crazy Tom–would build several "castles," but the aged Indian never spoke, and certainly never changed into a fair maiden.

To his death, in 1767, Tom continued to speak of Melvin the Great Enchanter and the old Indian woman. A letter written by him was discovered in 1835 in which he detailed the pursuit of his fantasy.

The remains of Crazy Tom's castles, heavy beams and sturdy stones, were later used to build a bridge over the Neshaminy Creek. And, the area where Crazy Tom's folly played out was changed to "Castle Valley."

The Pine Tree Farm B&B now stands on the site of Tom Meredith's old homestead.

The Hermit of Wolf Rocks

"Bert the Hermit" is how some folks referred to Albert Large, a gentlemen who made his mark on Bucks County history by leaving the rest of the world go by and retreating into his own refuge.

Born about 1805 in Buckingham Township, Albert was apparently intelligent and well-rounded. But while still in his teens, he fled not far from his home to Buckingham Mountain (a.k.a. Papcahesing, the "place of the woodpecker") and to Wolf Rocks, a rugged outcropping inside which he made his home for some four decades.

Any reliable details of this "Hermit of Wolf Rocks," as he was also known, are wildly speculative. Some reports claim that Albert Large was nothing more than a naturalist, an outdoorsman. He did not choose his lifestyle to shun civilization, but to embrace nature.

There was other evidence that Albert actually spent much time away from his hermitage. He would travel far at times, and would make many acquaintances in the world beyond the borders of Bucks County.

But, for many years, Albert Large simply did drop out of sight with those in the communities around him. It wasn't until April 9, 1858 that one mystery was solved and another was opened.

The day began when two men were scouring the hills in search of goats which had gone astray. As they approached what appeared to be a cave, they heard sounds from within it. They saw smoke coming from the rocks. They heard a voice.

They made their way into the tight confines of the cavern and came upon a man described as having "long gray hair in profusion" and a beard which "extended almost to his waist." That man was Albert Large.

Albert cautioned the men to come no farther, and indeed they fled in fear.

They solicited men from a nearby quarry and several went with them back to the cave. Upon hearing the heavy crowbars and tools clanking on his rockbound walls, Albert Large emerged, invited them in, and told them his story.

The men were flabbergasted, and soon the story of The Hermit of Wolf Rocks spread across Bucks and beyond. The news of the discovery of the recluse was reported in papers in America and abroad.

But then, as William C. Armstrong wrote in his *Albert Large, the Hermit Naturalist of Bucks County: A Biographical Sketch*, "No one knows what finally became of the hermit, whether he came back to civilization to die; or like the wild things, he searched out some quiet spot to die alone."

In his book, Armstrong relied heavily on information submitted to the Bucks County Historical Society by Col. Henry D. Paxson in 1895.

Paxson said, "After his discovery, Albert lingered about the mountain but a short time, and on yonder promontory he is said to have taken his farewell view of the beauty-woven valley and bade a silent but mournful adieu to those weird and romantic rocks.

"From thenceforth all traces of him and his later history have been lost."

Captain Kidd's Treasure –in Bucks County?

That heading should be enough to stir your curiosity a bit. And, I should add, there is only the slightest and wildest chance any of the pirate's loot is secreted anywhere in the soil of Bucks County, Pennsylvania.

And yet, there is an historical link between the captain and the county.

That link is John Bowman, as in Bowman's Hill.

Now a lovely spot where all may enjoy the beauty of the nearly 1,000 species of native wildflowers which grow on the hill and the trails which wind through meadows and woods, Bowman's Hill has been recognized as the

State Wildflower Preserve of Pennsylvania.

Founded in 1934, the 100-acre Bowman's Hill Wildflower Preserve shares the 500-foot high hill with a stone memorial tower built on the site of a Continental Army lookout position.

In 1696, John Bowman signed on as ship's surgeon in the fleet of Capt. William Kidd which was commissioned by the English government to rid the oceans of pirates who had been ravaging shipping.

The privateer turned pirate, and both the exploits of Captain Kidd on the high seas and the supposed treasures he and his crew buried along their wicked ways are the stuff of legends.

And, those legends extend–believe this or not–into the soil of Bucks County.

After Captain Kidd's crew disbanded in New York prior to Kidd's execution in 1700, John Bowman settled in Newtown. Somehow, he eventually made his way to a plot of land owned by Jonathan Pidcock on what was then Nenehawcachung, the natives' name for the hill.

As word of Bowman's piratical past filtered through the region, some believed he brought with him to that hill a share of treasure that he "earned" during the Captain Kidd years.

The rumor has never been substantiated–and, quite frankly, has probably no basis in truth whatsoever.

It is recorded, however, that "Doctor" Bowman was

buried on the eastern side of the hill, and therein dwells another legend.

In generations past, it was said that should you find Bowman's grave, kneel before it and repeat the question, "John Bowman...what killed you?" you will hear a disembodied voice whisper "*Nothing!*"

In documents on file in the Bucks County Historical Society, a retired steamboat captain named Aaron McCarty was interviewed at his small stone house at the foot of Bowman's Hill.

"One evening about nine o'clock," Capt. McCarty told a writer, "there was a rap at my door. Upon opening the door a total stranger presented himself and asked to be lodged overnight.

"He said he was a stranger to all of this region but seemed deeply interested.

"Finally he divulged the fact that his name was Bowman–a relative of Dr. John Bowman–and that his home was in western Pennsylvania. He said that Bowman's treasure is buried in the hill and that he had plans and diagrams at home that would probably lead to its discovery.

"He left with the avowed purpose of returning the next year with the drawings to look for the hidden gold. He never came, but word was finally received that his house was burned and he and the precious diagrams with it.

"So, if treasure there be, it still lies buried in the friendly bosom of the old hill."

In his "Historical Account of Bowman's Hill," Dr. J.E. Scott of New Hope addressed the lore and the lure of the hill.

"It is," Dr. Scott wrote, "to the student of folklore, of the weird, and uncanny that Bowman's Hill chiefly appeals.

"Traditions of pirates' buried treasure, of ghostly appearances...are as thick as leaves in Vallambrosa."

Dr. Scott then explained the John Bowman-as-pirate story, but with a twist typical of these kinds of legends.

"One story is that Dr. Bowman, surgeon in an English fleet sent out to capture Captain Kidd, turned pirate himself, as Kidd had previously done; joined that famous sea rover, and on his seizure in Boston sailed with his mates for the Capes of the Delaware, parted there from them, came up the river alone, died and at his own request was buried on the summit of the hill, where it was surmised by the treasure seekers he had previously buried his booty."

Is there buried treasure on Bowman's Hill? Does John Bowman's ghost guard it? If only in the ledgers of the legends of Bucks County, the answer to both question is yes.

•

The memorial tower atop Bowman's Hill.

BEWARE AT B. MAXWELL'S

Ghosts Abound in Downtown Doylestown Eatery

B. Maxwell's Restaurant, downtown Doylestown.

Maybe it only *seems* as if ghosts follow Mike Zoto anywhere he goes.

Consider this: Mike once owned the old Anchor Tavern, which, until it was destroyed by fire just prior to the publication of this book, was one of the oldest continuously-operating (since 1724) taverns in the county.

Situated near the intersection of routes 413 and the Second Street Pike, the Anchor was also well-known to be quite haunted.

Before we explore the ghost stories of B. Maxwell's in Doylestown, let us recall the ghosts of the old Anchor.

"It started with little things," Mike said. "I'd be closing up and my brother would be at the bar waiting for me and the television would just turn itself on."

Both men denied being anywhere near the TV or the remote, and both were baffled with that incident and several fairly common other unexplainable occurrences.

And then, there were the many experiences which were far from common.

"One server told us they had actually captured the image of a ghost on a picture of the fireplace. The picture was taken during a party, and there was an image in the picture that didn't belong," Mike continued.

"But the biggest things that happened were down in the basement," he added.

In fact, a team of paranormal researchers visited the Anchor in 1993, and after three hours of "reading" the building, they made an unnerving announcement.

"They told me that the basement was evil, really evil. They gave us significant details. They said there was a person in that basement that didn't want anybody in there, and that individual actually has chained-up women down there. He is very evil and a very violent ghost."

Mike said the horrid scene in the basement played out based on what the psychics said were actual events which took place there.

"We were always petrified down there," Zoto added. "There was a definite energy there."

But, the wicked spirit of the basement was not alone in the old inn.

"They also told me there was a German woman's ghost who made bread near what was the kitchen door," Zoto remembered.

Other spirits walled up inside the Anchor Tavern included a deceased maitre'd, and a host of ghosts in the third floor rooms of the old inn–ghosts which ranged from what was described as a fugitive in hiding to a forlorn bride and groom on an eternal honeymoon.

But, alas, the Anchor Tavern is no more. At the time of the publication of this volume, nature had begun to claim all but the paved parking lot of the fire-raved tavern.

And thus, the ghosts have too disappeared.

Or have they?

Most students of the paranormal believe that although the *physical* structure–the Anchor Tavern–has been destroyed, the *psychic* energy may well remain on and in the land upon which it took its form.

And so, could it be that those ghosts still reside on that empty lot? Only time–and perhaps whoever occupies the site in the future–will tell.

Mike Zoto went on to purchase the landmark eatery in downtown Doylestown known as B. Maxwell's. And, with his new challenge came new ghosts.

"I've had experiences here," Mike said within the lovely high Victorian confines of B. Maxwell's, "but not as profound as at the Anchor.

"I know others have had many encounters, and I can say that in the early 1900s, someone did hang themself in the basement.

"Even though it was a man who hanged himself down there, it's a woman's ghost–I think her name is Rosemary–that haunts this place."

As our research and interviews at B. Maxwell's broadened, we discovered that "Rosemary" is not alone in the swirl of energy inside the restaurant.

Bonnie Cooke took time from her work at B. Maxwell's to discuss her experiences at the restaurant.

As for who haunts the place: "We have two ghosts,"

she said.

Bonnie believes the spirits are those of a husband and wife who resided in the building during its earliest years.

"I saw her twice," Bonnie stated. "I saw a cream-colored dress go by the door and I went looking for either the hostess or the bartender, but there was nobody there.

"Later, I was up in the second floor in the employees' break kitchen. I glanced over and saw someone sitting there, and then I heard someone sigh. But I was alone at the time!"

Others, including employees and patrons, have reported glimpses of unidentifiable passers-by.

Several employees said they have heard their names called by a hushed, female voice. Others say they distinctly heard someone whisper, "Excuse me..." when there was nobody else around.

Some who work there said the most "activity" seems to take place near the telephones on the second floor and throughout the third floor.

Ginny Eismann, day supervisor at B. Maxwell's at the time of our visit, offered a story that had unfolded only weeks before the interview.

"Our manager was at the register on the first floor and had just put down the receipts for the night. He was distracted and turned. As he looked back, though, all the receipts were gone.

"He looked through everything and couldn't find them. He even looked in the reservation book. He was getting madder by the minute. He ripped the whole place apart!

"He went away for a few seconds and came back. There they were, right on top of his books. He blamed it on the ghost, of course.

"He said, 'you idiot!' And as he said that, he swore on his mother's life, that standing in front of him was an old woman, sunken eye sockets, curly black hair, an old apron, and an old-fashioned green and white dress.

"When he called her an idiot, she just briefly appeared and then disappeared!

"Apparently, at that point, he had made her mad. So he took all his business cash and receipts up to the office on the third floor and sat there putting his money and receipts away.

"And then, the door opened and shut...opened and shut...ten times! Bang! Ten times!"

Another time, Ginny said, an employee said he saw a brown jacket disengage itself from a coat rack and float over his head.

B. Maxwell's has drawn excellent reviews for what one critic called its comfortable, "museum-like decor."

As for its pesky ghosts, Mike Zoto is unfazed. After all, despite the occasional phantom whispers and unexplained apparition, he and most folks who work there take it all in stride.

"Nothing bad has ever happened here," he said. "Just recently I was in my office at around nine o'clock at night, and I heard someone walking back and forth. My assistant manager was in the next room, but was working at a desk.

"I asked her if she was walking, and she said no.

"She said it was probably just *her*, visiting us again."

•

I SEE HER!

The Ghost of Chef Tell's Manor House

A canal-side view of Chef Tell's Manor House.

In the world of the culinary arts, in the greater Philadelphia area, and certainly in Bucks County, Friedman Paul Erhardt needs no introduction.

His strapping appearance, his renowned wit, and his signature "I See You!" have endeared him to millions of people through his appearances on regional and national television as "Chef Tell," an ambassador of good cooking and hearty eating.

Born in 1943 in Stuttgart, Chef Tell became a "Master Chef" before he was 30–the youngest chef ever in West Germany to earn that title.

After winning several gold medals for his culinary skills, after becoming Chef of the Year in Germany, after receiving a masters degree in cooking from the University of Heidelberg, after winning four Cordon Bleu awards, and after winning the hearts and tummies of diners throughout Europe, Tell Erhardt became head chef at the Marriott Hotel in Philadelphia.

When he decided to establish his own restaurant, he decided to do so in Bucks County.

Little did he know that with his elegant canalside inn near Upper Black Eddy would come a ghost.

"Oh, yes," Chef Tell told us in his engaging German accent, "we have a woman here.

"She opens doors, and does many other things."

Chef Tell's Manor House is tucked tightly between Route 32 and the canal, and it was along that waterway that Chef Tell was told a tragedy once unfolded.

"Apparently, there was a house of ill repute on the second floor here at one time," he told us. "And, from what I heard, there was a woman up there 'taking care of business' while her two and a half year old child roamed around and drowned in the canal."

Erhardt, and others, believe the ghost of that mother now roams the inn and the edge of the canal in hopes of a spirit reunion with her child.

The inn was built around 1830, and Chef Tell believes the incident which sparked the ghostly perambulations took place in the late 19th century.

Most of what the chef can attribute only to the unexplainable took place early in his ownership of the Manor House.

"Once in a while," he said, "we'd be sitting here late at night and the men's room door would open and close on its own.

"We'd hear squeaking sounds, and sometimes things got moved around up on the second floor."

While he noted drastic swings in temperatures on the second floor, Chef Tell also said the forlorn spirit has never done anything harmful.

Waiter Eric Cutting agreed, but did admit he's felt uncomfortable at times.

"I heard my name being called at times–mostly upstairs–and when I turned around, there'd be nobody there, things like that," he told us.

On one occasion, a team of painters working on the third floor told Erhardt that they felt a "presence" on the third floor. To assuage their discomfort, they placed a crucifix in the room, to fend off the ghost.

One investigator confirmed that there was the rather strong energy of a young woman inside the Manor House, and that a lesser spirit seemed to glide along the banks of the canal to the rear of the restaurant. That is believed to be the ghost of the little girl who drowned.

The spirit which roams the canal seems, in the medium's words, "terribly confused, very sad, and quite unprepared for the horror which was inflicted on it at such a young, innocent age."

•

THE PROTECTIVE GHOST

A "Good Ghost" Keeps Watch at the Pineville Tavern

The Pineville Tavern, Pineville.

A view of the Pineville Tavern from the outside does not do justice to what one will find inside.

What's inside is a warren of cozy chambers which range from a standard neighborhood roadhouse barroom to some of the most atmospheric, rustic settings of any restaurant in Bucks County.

In the oldest section, which dates to 1742, a fieldstone hearth stands guard over pumpkin pine flooring, ancient, dimly-lit walls, and a collection of collectibles which almost appear to have been placed to achieve a desired effect.

And indeed, they were!

Andrew Abruzzese, owner of the restaurant, is a painting contractor by trade. And, with a keen eye toward making his establishment inviting and intriguing, he actually commissioned a theatrical set designer to create the atmosphere and seamlessly blend the 1742 room with the "newer" 1793 portion and other later additions.

There is documentation which confirms that while the oldest section may have actually been built as a residence, the building was the center of much trade and commerce along the Durham Road from its very beginnings and evolved into the Pineville Hotel.

There's an interesting, somewhat schizophrenic, geopolitical quirk about the Pineville Tavern. When you walk through the front door you're in Buckingham

Township. But, should you choose to dine in one of the back rooms, you will do so in Wrightstown Township.

As for ghosts, Andrew is at once philosophical and receptive.

"After all," he said, "it *is* a 280-year old building!"

Before, during, and since his meticulous restoration of the old hotel, Andrew said some rather odd occurrences led several people at the Pineville Tavern to believe they were being watched over by a benign spirit.

"I truly believe it is a protective ghost," Andrew stated. "No one has ever had a bad experience. I think the energy here gives us warnings that something's about to happen. The modern history of this place has been all good karma."

Ruth Brennan, an employee at the tavern, remembered an unsolicited and unexpected revelation from a recent customer.

"We had a psychic who came here and told me the energy was strongest back in here," Ruth said as we stood in the 1742 room. "And," she continued, "they said it was also quite strong in the basement."

The psychic, Ruth added, also told her the energy was most likely that of a former resident.

Our own research revealed that the presence seems to be that of a burly individual, probably male, who seems to carry a large parcel or package in an eternal stroll through the rear dining rooms and through a doorway which may have existed prior to the renovations and connection of the old and new sections.

Innocuous and oblivious to any present-day activities which swirl throughout the busy restaurant, the energy seems to be that of the ghost of someone who may have been a farmhand or laborer. His load may well be a bale of hay or sack of grain.

Andrew Abruzzese fully acknowledges the observations of some employees and several guests who believe a ghost strolls in their midst.

"Some customers take the ghost very seriously," he said. "And I think there is something to it."

Andrew does not claim to have ever seen the spirit, but he is quite at home with whatever is there and gives back-handed credit to the energy it generates.

There was a rash of false fire alarms touched off at the tavern just prior to our interview, and the staff blamed it, of course, on *the ghost*.

Andrew wasn't quite as whimsical and flippant about the situation.

"I feel that whoever, or whatever, is here set off the alarm to keep us on our toes," he said.

"It's more than an energy. It's definitely a feeling that there's somebody–or something–here, on our side."

CHILDREN OF THE NIGHT

Youthful Pair Play Eternally at the Temperance House

Sam Willard, Bill Hollowell and Chillion Higgs would never recognize the place.

Well, they may recognize some of the physical attributes of The Temperance House, but they'd be downright appalled at what's going on there these days!

Situated in the very heart of the Newtown Historic District, The Temperance House has been serving travelers and locals since 1772 when Andrew and Nancy McMinn established a combination school and tavern on the State Street site.

For more than six decades, the inn grew, served many keepers, and hosted everyone from common teamsters to colonial generals.

In 1835, Newtown constable Chillion W. Higgs purchased the place and put an end to the serving of anything stronger than lemonade, cider, and mineral water. Higgs' "The Sign of the Good Samaritan" was, in his words, "where the Temperance man could find accommodation for himself and his horse."

And so it was. For 130 years, The Temperance House was dry–except for the soft drinks and ice cream it became known for.

Thanks to an 1840s sign out front with a deer

standing by Niagara Falls, the inn was sometimes known as the *Niagara* Temperance House. And, the painter of that sign, the teetotalling Quaker and Newtown resident Edward Hicks, went on to become a renowned primitive artist whose work is now considered to be classic Americana. Hicks, who moved from Langhorne to Newtown in 1811, and his Peaceable Kingdom series, painted between the early 1820s and 1849, are true museum pieces.

When Hicks, a Quaker minister who established the Friends meeting in Newtown, died in 1849, an estimated 4,000 people turned out for his funeral in town.

The serving of liquor and beer didn't resume at The Temperance House until 1963 when H. Clifton Neff bought the establishment and turned on the taps.

In 1985, more than $1.5 million were pumped into a massive restoration of the 13-room inn, and The Temperance House fulfilled a destiny Andy and Nancy McMinn could hardly have imagined.

The inn itself is now classic Americana, and the setting for a most interesting ghost story.

"There have been about six sightings of them," said Jim Calderone, owner of The Temperance House. "There are two colonial-era children. They seem to hang around mostly in the hallway. They just seem to frolic around, being mischievous, like kids!"

Several independent on-site investigations have all

come to the same conclusion. There are two young spirits–a boy and a girl–and no apparent baseline for the haunting.

Jim said that just after the 1985 renovations, the energy seemed to be at its strongest.

And, that energy often manifested itself in rather unnerving fashion.

"A couple was here on their honeymoon," Jim said. "They told me that the two children scampered through their room in the middle of the night. When they described what they had experienced, it was exactly what a medium had previously told me happened there."

Jim is not hesitant about naming the specific rooms where ghostly activity has been reported. The are Edward Hicks Suite, the Chillion Higgs Room, the Benetz Suite, and the Twining Room.

While most encounters with the energy have been fairly benign, there was one rather disturbing incident–disturbing, at least, to the handyman who experienced it.

A housekeeper had just tidied up the Chillion Higgs Room and called for the handyman to come and do some minor work in the room.

The gent opened the door into the room and witnessed what he later described as a ghostly little girl jumping on the freshly-made bed.

Ann Hoffman, manager of The Temperance House,

recalled the event.

"He told the girl that a nice lady just fixed that bed. He told her she'd better stop jumping or she'd be in trouble." After his warning, the jumping did stop–and the little girl vanished.

Later, the housekeeper confirmed the story.

Ann said she has had some unexplainable experiences in the old inn. She has actually witnessed an upstairs window opening–three times–with no human aid. She has felt an invisible force around her, seemingly protecting her.

On one quiet moment in one of the rooms, she felt as if someone was stroking her cheek and humming softly.

"I never feel any negative energy," she noted. "It's always a feeling of warmth. That's why I think it's the children."

"We have had folks report the sound of children laughing and bouncing a ball in certain rooms and in the halls upstairs," she added.

And with all that, does Jim or Ann, or anyone who's ever stayed there or worked there feel as if they'd like to flee in fear?

Never. Even the couple who had their honeymoon interrupted never complained.

Ann Hoffman agrees. "I'm truly fascinated by it all. I just love being in here!"

THE DANCING GHOST OF BRISTOL

Dapper Ghost Prances at the King George II Inn

The King George II Inn, Bristol.

The tangle of highways in lower Bucks County smoothes out by the time one reaches the revitalized riverfront of historic Bristol.

There, along Radcliffe and some connecting streets are stately homes and buildings which recall the days when Bristol bristled with activity as a ferry port, a canal depot, a market town, and even a spa resort.

Then as now, the long strand of the Delaware River at Bristol plays an important role in the borough's economic and spiritual well-being.

One particular place on the Bristol riverfront stands out for its role in a history which dates as far back as 1681.

The King George II Inn claims to be the oldest

continuously operated inn in America. It has been hailed as one of the most "romantic" restaurants in the county and as one of the finest restaurants in the entire country.

And, it may have a ghost or two roaming its fine dining rooms, basement, and upper floors.

Jeff Brenner is general manager of the King George II, and he has several stories about odd encounters in the big building.

He speaks of unspeakable acts which were said to have taken place in the dark confines of the basement. He said it was once a jail and for whatever reason, some employees there are quite hesitant to venture into the area alone–or at all!

Jeff tells of a step-sister who lived in an upstairs room for a while and reported the distinct sound of a baby crying deep within the walls of the old inn. She, Jeff says, swore it was the weeping of an infant's ghost.

Eerie sounds and unexplained sights are fairly commonplace in the King George II, and never has anyone been anything more than "spooked" by them.

Jeff himself can never adequately explain something he witnessed a while back at the inn.

"We have an in-house security system. I went into the office one night and I heard something.

"I checked the video monitor for the third floor, and I saw a man, wearing a top hat, dancing around. It looked like he was intoxicated. He was having a good time up there, all by himself."

Now, some of you more "seasoned" readers may recognize Bristol as the setting for a bit of dance and music history. It was where a Philadelphia record promoter picked up on a dance the kids in Bristol were doing at the Goodwill Fire Hall in 1960.

Soon adapted to music, "The Bristol Stomp" became a big hit for the Dovells and carried the borough's name into pop music immortality.

Was this gent doing the "Bristol Stomp" up there on the third floor of the King George II? Not likely.

"The image was fuzzy," Jeff Brenner says. He remembers that as he looked more closely he could tell the figure was not an actual, living person. There are tenants in upstairs rooms, but this top-hatted individual was not one of them.

He feels it was someone perhaps of that place, but not of this time. "He looked like someone from the 19th century," Jeff adds.

He looked like a dapper, dancing ghost.

•

THE PRACTICAL JOKER GHOST

Oddities in the Ottsville Inn

Scott Burns–now there's a name for a Scotsman. And a true Scotsman Scott is. A former pub owner and businessman in his native land, Scott has owned and lived in the Ottsville Inn since the late 1980s.

And through a lilting brogue he told us of the unexplainable events which have led him and others to believe that the old inn along the old Durham Road is inhabited by a *bogle* or two.

"He appears to us to be a funny ghost," Scott said. "He's very playful."

Mostly, whatever energy may dwell in the building plays tricks on unsuspecting victims. It moves things, hides things, toys with things.

"Even to the point," Scott continued as he held an oversized pepper mill in his hand, "that this very pepper mill once disappeared."

Light switches flip themselves off for no apparent reason. It's not just that the *lights* go off, mind you, but the entire light *switch*–which normally takes a certain amount of pressure to "flick," flicks.

Scott says previous owners told him they had similar experiences in the place. And, the manifestations of this playful ghost have transcended tomfoolery.

"If you're sitting here during the day," Scott added,

"you're sometimes distracted because you know something has walked across the dining room.

"A customer might be sitting at the corner of the bar and look around, as if there is somebody in the hallway, and there isn't."

As the spirit in the Ottsville Inn has made itself known, its mischievous antics have even sparked brief family arguments. But, Scott said everyone who has crossed the eternal path of the ghost has had to admit that there's an unearthly aura about the place at times.

"Either my wife or I will be sitting here alone and we'll get a clear, distinct sense of something walking around. We look around to see who it is, and there's no one.

"It's as if someone came in the door, but no one did!"

As a place where canal workers congregated and as the focal point of activity in one of the oldest settlements in upper Bucks, the Ottsville Inn may well be the perfect host for its playful ghost.

•

ON A MISSION...

Familiar Spirit Returns Often to the Cascade Lodge

The Cascade Lodge.

When Sandy Knuth spent her first night in the Cascade Lodge in the 1970s, she fell asleep easily, but sometime in the night she felt something shaking her, waking her.

She awoke to the smell of smoke. She awakened her husband in time to search the lodge, discover a pile of smoldering rags and avert a potential disaster.

"From that moment," Sandy said, "I felt there was a spirit here. A protective spirit."

As the wife of the man whose family had founded the stunning restaurant along Lehnenberg Road near Kintnersville in 1939, Sandy is rightfully proud of the elegant dining rooms, lounges, and function rooms of the Cascade Lodge. And, she graciously accepts the fact that within those rooms glides ghostly energy.

"I lived in houses before where there were ghosts," she said. "It's nothing new to me."

Footsteps on empty stairs, pockets of air pressure, water spigots turning themselves on and off–nothing new to Sandy Knuth.

"Here," she continued, "you can feel it–the spirit–walk up the steps with you."

Others who have spent many years on the staff of the highly-regarded restaurant agree that there are benevolent spirits in the many rooms of the lodge.

Dawn Young, who is a believer in ghosts and an occupant of a home she says has a presence in it, has witnessed water faucets turning themselves on and off in the Cascade Lodge. She has heard the distinctive crunching sound of someone walking on floor mats in the basement–when she knew no one was *in* the basement. "I've never seen anything here," the 13-year employee told us, "but I can definitely feel the presence."

Peggy Petner, who has worked at the lodge for 15 years, has heard footsteps creaking their way up a staircase, and once stood near a light which, with no human aid, switched itself on.

Sandy Knuth said even casual observers who come to the Cascade Lodge to experience its fine cuisine are often greeted with surprises.

"One time, a woman and I were coming out of the ladies room when she went 'whooo!'

"I asked her what was the matter. She told me she got the sensation that someone had just passed in back of her. She said she felt it was female.

"Then, she asked me if our place was haunted.

"I said, 'yes!'"

That place, the Cascade Lodge, is reminiscent of a manor house in Britain as it looks over the rolling hills which spread beneath its stately walls.

It was Sandy Knuth's father-in-law, Capt. Ernest Knuth, who opened the lodge in these quiet hills of upper Bucks.

Ernest had chosen the sailing life after leaving a comfortable childhood in his native Denmark. He trained at the Danish Nautical Academy and later became a captain in the United States Merchant Marine.

During a stopover in Hoboken, New Jersey in 1926 he met and married a German immigrant named Paula Uhl. He retired from the Merchant Marine and he and she began a second career in the restaurant business.

Their first restaurant was in Brooklyn. But Ernest and Paula longed for a life in the country. In 1935, they bought a colonial-era Pennsylvania farmhouse which was positioned near natural springs which cascaded down the hillside. Thus, the name for their dream lodge–the *Cascade* Lodge.

Captain Knuth passed away in the 1950s, but some people believe his spirit may still oversee the operations of the lodge, which is now in the hands of his son, Howard, and his wife, Sandy.

Sandy said many "sensitives" have come to the Cascade Lodge and before they left, have volunteered their observations of spirit energy in areas which range from the old dining room to a linen closet.

On one occasion, a medium told Sandy that there was one very strong spirit which inhabits a corner of the dining room.

"And," said Sandy, "she told me he's a flirt!

"She said she couldn't actually see him, but was

positive he was there."

Another individual claimed there were three ghosts roaming the Cascade Lodge at any given time. "One," Sandy remembered, "was thought to be from the Revolutionary War time, and the other two were from a later period. There were two men and a woman. The medium said that whoever they were, they like to have a lot of fun and they particularly like that old dining room, in the original part of the house."

No matter how many self-proclaimed "mediums" or "sensitives" may tell their tales, Sandy believes that only one reading of the ghostly energy in the lodge is irrefutable–her own.

"One night I was sleeping upstairs and I happened to look up and I saw the gentleman standing there, looking at me," she said.

"Of course, I got scared," she continued, "but I was more startled than anything else."

And who was, or is, *the gentleman*?

Without hesitation, Sandy answered: "It's my father-in-law. That's who it is."

Sandy has never come across the two other ghosts that one medium claimed were in the lodge. "But my father-in-law is here. If there really are two others, I've never seen them and I have no idea who they are."

So, could that "flirtatious" ghost who surfaced for another medium be Capt. Knuth?

"Oh, yes," Sandy said with a giggle. "He *was* a flirt. He was a sea captain, and very definitely a fun-loving person...and a flirt."

The captain has made his presence known to a few others in the lodge, including a cleaning lady who told Sandy he actually spoke to her.

"He said he has a mission to do every so often," Sandy related. "He goes and does his mission and comes back here. When he comes back, he says it's good to be home."

Sandy feels that while he may be somewhat of a flirt, and may kick up a little spooky dust every once in a while, the gentleman–the captain–adds a kind of charm to the lodge.

"For some reason," she said, "this place does seem to have its own *being*, its own *spirit*. There's something here that makes people feel very much at home when they walk in."

•

Researcher David J. Seibold stands at a doorway where ghosts have been spotted at the Cascade Lodge.

MIMI

Flowery Aroma Portends Arrival of Ghost at Odette's

Odette's, just south of New Hope.

Odette's needs little introduction to anyone who has ever passed through Bucks County.

Situated on a sliver of land between the river and the canal just south of New Hope, it is a world-class restaurant and cabaret which has been attracting a discriminating clientele for several decades.

The ambience and elegance of the present Odette's was not always the hallmark at what was once known as the River House.

The earliest tavern stood on the site in 1794. Its position at the head of dangerous rapids known as Wells Falls made it a convenient watering hole for riverboat pilots and skippers.

In the early 19th century, it served a boisterous bunch of boatmen who dropped in as their canal barges traversed the New Hope locks of the Delaware Canal. When an outlet lock was built nearby in 1854 to shunt barges into the river to connect with the Delaware and Raritan Canal on the New Jersey side, the River House was isolated on its little island.

As the fortunes of the canal ebbed, so did the fate of the River House. After several years of a downward spiral, the building was reborn as the first tourist hotel in New Hope during the town's burgeoning years as an arts and tourism center in the 1930s.

The venerable hostelry began to take its present form and name when Parisian-born Odette Myrtil retired from a stellar career on Broadway and in Hollywood and opened "Chez Odette" as a top-shelf French restaurant.

Odette Myrtil may still be seen on celluloid in more than two dozen films. Among them, the 1942 James Cagney classic "Yankee Doodle Dandy" and the 1951 Alfred Hitchcock thriller "Strangers On A Train." In the latter, look for Odette as Madame Darville.

And, it would be quite convenient if the spirit of Mme. Odette could still be seen, so to speak, at her old *bistro*. But alas, such is not the case.

There is no evidence that Odette's ghost remained in the restaurant after her death in 1978. Nor have there been any reports of the ghost of another prominent woman whose name is forever attached to Odette's.

Chester County's gift to network TV, Jessica Savitch, was killed when her car plummeted into the canal on a foggy night in 1983. She was 36, and had been sorting out her life after stormy personal and professional times.

Many psychics, mediums, and dabblers in the paranormal have offered their opinions and observations as to what and who haunts Odette's, but no one has ever offered anything of substance which could identify the ghosts.

But one thing is for certain–Odette's is, in the classic sense of the word–haunted.

"Yes," said proprietor Diane Barbone Guzzardo, "I do believe there are ghosts in the building."

Quite aware of and enlightened about such matters, Diane said she has never detected any hostilities, but has most certainly had her brushes with the energies and entities of Odette's.

"There is a presence which sometimes walks to the third floor," she explained. "I would say the third floor is not a good feeling. That's the doorway that, at times, I turn and walk away from.

"I've never had a sense of who the ghost might be," she added. "It could have been as far back as the barge men who used to come in here, or the dancing girls, who knows?

"There is one picture of Odette here that seems to stare out. I had my puppy in here once and when it walked past that one picture of Odette, it started to bark at it! I hid it in the ladies' room."

Diane has had many reports from members of the staff regarding their own encounters with the unknown.

"My secretary, for example, was in the office and somebody–a male voice–said hello to her. She turned around and expected to find someone, and there was no one," she said.

And while that secretary, that time, heard that *male* voice, others who work at Odette's seem to think the dominant spirit there is a woman. And, they even have a name for her.

"A couple came in here years ago," said Kathie

Brydzinski, a longtime server a Odette's. "They said they were psychics. They said there was a woman by the name of Mimi who was murdered in the back bar. They said she occupied one particular booth there. She is our ghost."

Kathie said she believes Mimi was an employee there at one time, but would not hazard a guess as to when. "It gets weird at times," she continued. "One night I was back in the area where 'Mimi' is supposed to be. There were people seated at 'Mimi's' table, and the door back there slammed shut. They said it was the wind, but I didn't think so. I still cringe when people sit at that table.

"Lights flicker, and I smell flowers everywhere," she added.

And, Kathie agrees with Diane that the third floor is the least inviting section of the building. "It's a cold feeling, like something might have happened up there. It's just a feeling I get. Sometimes it's as if somebody's touching my hair, sort of."

Another server at Odette's, Helen Schaeffer, believes there are two spirits. One is a resolute masculine ghost, the other is an equally headstrong feminine spirit.

"My first experience was when I had just started and I was in the kitchen. I heard my name being called. It freaked me out. I had to go all the way back to the walk-in, and I was scared. So, I ran.

"Then, when I came back I heard my name again and there was nobody in the kitchen. That ghost was in that kitchen. I actually screamed!

"Another time, on the second floor, I glanced into a very big mirror. I swear I saw shadows walking past that mirror. And that's happened a couple times over the years."

Helen said she has been told by customers that they have actually photographed unexplainable anomalies while taking pictures at Odette's. "In fact," Helen recalled, "a few years ago a chef was coming out of the tunnel from the kitchen and he told me he saw the spirit of a man in the theater room."

And, there's always *that* feeling that someone's there, just beyond your eyesight, just over your shoulder.

"Many times, you'll get that feeling," Helen said. "But it's good. It's as if the spirits are protecting us. I'm never afraid here."

Another employee at Odette's said she has often sniffed a burst of a flowery aroma and within minutes experienced something odd and unexplainable. "Mimi was there," she shrugged.

Diane Barbone Guzzardo, who has maintained her family's proud traditions at Odette's for the last several years, said that if the ghost is indeed "Mimi," then so be it.

"Who knows? Mimi could have been a barmaid here a century ago, or one of the dancing girls. It's been a functioning tavern for a long, long time," she said.

Diane has a sense of humor and a sense of adventure about the spirits of Odette's.

What's more, she remains receptive to the reality that there is a darned good, old-fashioned ghost mystery within the walls of a true Bucks County landmark.

•

Main Street, New Hope, seen in a vintage post card view.

THE CIGARETTE-SMOKING GHOST

Former Innkeeper Still Puffs Away at Hulmeville Inn

Once upon a time, the Hulmeville Inn was Marek's Cafe, a "shot-and-a-beer" kind of place where Tony Marek held court either from behind the bar or on his big easy chair.

Tony was beloved by just about anybody who stopped in. During World War II, Tony was in the hosiery business in California. Then, he came east to help his mother run the bar in lower Bucks–and he never left the place.

Literally.

For years since Tony's death in the tavern in 1984, customers and employees have been experiencing several phenomena and blaming Tony's ghost.

A light switches on–or off–on its own: Tony.

The sound of shoes shuffle on an empty floor: Tony.

A pungent smell of cigarette smoke wafts from where nobody is smoking: Tony.

Jim Lavin owns the century-old inn with his father, Don, and fully recognizes the probability that the Hulmeville Inn is haunted. His own experiences have been minimal, but he did relate stories of how chairs seem to relocate themselves mysteriously and of how several deliverymen have reported odd encounters with unseen forces.

"Every once in a while," he said, "one of our bartenders would say that they felt something strange back there. We hear feet shuffling, and in the basement there's a faint aroma of cigarette smoke. Supposedly, that's Tony coming back."

Jackie Meyer has tended bar at the Hulmeville Inn, in her words, "Forever...longer than the ghost!"

She lives across the street from the inn and admitted that she has had some peculiar experiences over the years. "I've had what I call 'light' experiences, as in lights going on and off–things like that."

She reiterated that Tony's bar was a neighborhood gathering place for a more mature crowd. She said Tony loved to hunt and fish and spin yarns about his many travels around the world.

Now, the Hulmeville Inn attracts a much younger clientele. As Jackie quipped, "Maybe Tony's upset that there's a couple hundred 24-year olds hanging around, interrupting his fishing shows and whatever!"

So, what would Tony Marek's family think of the prospect of his ghost lingering in his old barroom?

Actually, they're fine with it–at least his daughter, Mary Ellen (Marek) Jackson is.

"I have stories that will back it all up," Mary Ellen said. "One day, I was working around the kitchen and the guy who cleans the coils for the beer system came up from the basement and told me I'd better get down there because he smelled smoke.

"I said, oh, there's no smoke. That's just my dad. So I went back into the kitchen. He came back a few minutes later, a little ashen, and asked me if my dad was dead. I said yes, and that he used to go downstairs and sneak a smoke. So, I told him it was just Tony down there sneaking a smoke. Well, this kid turned purple!"

Mary said neither she nor anyone she knows has actually seen her father in spirit form, but his distinct aroma has led even the most unsuspecting, unprepared, and unbelieving folks to take notice.

"My husband, who's not the least bit interested in anything supernatural, came home one night and woke me up. He said, 'you're not going to believe this, but I was cleaning up back in the kitchen and I could smell your dad back there.'

"I just laughed. Then, he told me it wasn't the first time, either. He told me it had happened before," Mary said.

Those other times, Mary's husband shrugged off the notion that Tony's presence may still be there. "But that one time," Mary added, "he just looked at me and said 'Your dad was in that kitchen.'"

"Yeah," Mary said, "we kind of think he is!"

•

THE CHRISTMAS EVE GHOST

...of Pen Ryn Mansion

Williamsburg and Jamestown, Virginia, have their plantations along the James River. Philadelphia and Bucks County have their Mansions Along the Delaware.

From Glenfoerd to Pennsbury, and in between and beyond, several stately colonial manor houses surrounded by sprawling riverside estates once defined the Pennsylvania shoreline of the busy Delaware River.

Among those which have survived the centuries is the magnificent Pen Ryn Mansion in Bensalem.

Set on 100 acres, the mansion faces gardens and lawns which lead to the river bank. And, despite its bucolic beauty of today, Pen Ryn once faced a dire fate.

The central portion of the mansion is the oldest, built in 1744 by Philadelphia shipping magnate Abraham Bickley. Later additions were built in the 1890s at the instruction of Lucy Wharton Drexel, heir to vast family fortunes. During her ownership, the carriage house, staff quarters, art gallery, and library were added.

And, for the better part of a century, Pen Ryn Mansion prospered as a residence and then a school until hard times hit and the property fell into disrepair.

From 1988 to 1993, it was abandoned and nearly laid to waste.

With a massive infusion of money and

entrepreneurship, Pen Ryn was purchased, restored, refurbished, and expanded as a high-class banquet and conference facility. It also qualified to be listed on the National Register of Historic Places.

Bill Haas, proprietor of Pen Ryn Mansion, called it "A house that's had nine lives."

And, Mr. Haas added that the gorgeous building–a favorite site for weddings and receptions–also has a ghost story attached to it.

Among the many offerings of the mansion are group tours which, according to the brochure, "are filled with stories of intrigue and romance that relate to the Bickley and Drexel families, Ben Franklin, Benjamin West, and even...a Christmas Eve ghost!"

"To my knowledge," Mr. Haas told us, "although I haven't seen any complete, documented records, there were seven Bickley children, all of whom lived and died here unmarried.

"They were all Tory sympathizers to the point that they helped finance the British against the Colonists. They were wealthy shipping merchants.

"I believe it was Robert Bickley who had intentions to marry a colonial woman. He brought her home one Christmas Eve to Pen Ryn to meet the rest of the family.

"Well, the father, Abraham Bickley, was so upset that he got in a heated argument with his son.

"Robert then ran down to the river, threw himself

into the icy Delaware River, and disappeared forever."

Then again, according to local legend and several eyewitnesses, that is perhaps not quite true.

It is said that after the blowup between father and son, Abraham Bickley became quite upset with himself. His son had walked away from his rage several times before, but had always returned.

So, when Abraham Bickley heard a loud rapping at his front door a while after Robert left, he breathed a sigh of relief and knew it was his son returning. Surely, they would talk things out and resolve their dispute.

But, to the elder Bickley's shock and confusion, when he opened the door that cold Christmas Eve, no one was there.

There have been reports of this episode playing out several times at Pen Ryn, and not just on Christmas Eve. A loud knock on the front door will be heard, and when someone answers it they find nothing–but they hear a distant moaning, grumbling sound.

On occasion, they may see the misty form of a drenched man in an ancient, tattered cloak, appear and then disappear in the night.

A resident of a property near Pen Ryn said he was told by an individual who worked at the mansion before its most recent restoration that he had heard knocks on the door and tappings on the windows several times. Each time, he replied, "Robert, go away." And, the tappings and knockings stopped.

"Supposedly," Bill Haas continued, "every Christmas Eve the ghost comes back and taps on the windows."

Haas has been at the mansion three Christmas Eves and has never seen nor heard the ghost.

But, the mansion does honor Robert Bickley's legend and maintains a vigil for his return every Christmas Eve.

There is a certain irony that this modern transformation of Pen Ryn as a showpiece of festive and romantic events should have a ghost story rooted in a tragic love affair.

Maybe, Robert's restless and forlorn spirit returns to draw from the mansion the passion and understanding which eluded him in life.

Bill Haas is philosophical about the matter. "Any ghost who has survived everything this place has been through over the centuries can't be a bad ghost," he reasoned.

SWEET AROMA PORTENDS GHOST

The Ghost of Bucks County Community College's Tyler Hall

Tyler Hall, Bucks County Community College.

We walked past the four stone cottages which once housed the gardener, chauffeurs, and butler. We strolled between garish brick buildings which are so very necessary but so very out of place.

We passed by the Cooper Homestead building, which has miraculously survived as a modern college campus grew around it.

We saw The Orangery, and marveled at the awkward juxtaposition of styles and periods in the heart of what is now Bucks County Community College–known affectionately as BC3.

Over the stone shoulders of the homestead building, a satellite dish. Next to The Orangery, a confusing abstract "sculpture." All around us, a bit of history.

Before the modern buildings of BC3 rose upon which legend has it was a "council rock" where natives gathered, the campus and some 1,700 acres of state park around it were owned by George and Stella Tyler.

Hence, the names of the surrounding Tyler State Park and our destination that day–Tyler Hall.

Tyler Hall is the nerve center and signature building of BC3. And, if the many tales told by many students, staff, and faculty members are to be believed, Tyler Hall is haunted by a quite benign and benevolent spirit.

Our guide through the campus was Sandra Sobek-Allen, a security guard at BC3 since 1989. Once inside

Tyler hall, she ushered us through a complex of modern college offices, work rooms, and food service areas until we emerged into the Dining Room.

Along the way, we passed a portrait of the elegant Stella Tyler. An accomplished businesswoman, sculptor, and patron of arts and education, Stella Tyler bequeathed her beloved mansion and land to Temple University in 1962. The Bucks County Commissioners purchased the property in 1964 as the site for the county's Community College.

Ghostly stories started to be told in the earliest years of the conversion from mansion to campus. Since then, several generations of students have been introduced to the inexplicable events which manifest within the two-foot thick, cork-insulated walls of Tyler Hall.

It didn't take Sandra Sobek-Allen long to become acquainted with the stories–and whom she believes is the subject of those stories.

In fact, it was on her very first overnight shift as a campus security guard when she was introduced to the unexplainable.

"I had come into the dining room through the door from the kitchen," she remembered. "The room was empty, the whole building was empty.

"And then, I heard someone walk in. I said 'hold on, I'll be right with you.' Then, there was like a film in the room and I felt a presence. I didn't see it, but I felt it. And, I definitely heard someone come through that door–that *locked* door!"

Sandra thought it might be a maintenance worker. But when she looked, and looked again, she saw she was alone.

As we continued our stroll through what was once a 45-room French-Norman home, we marveled at the intricate woodwork, the art, and the beauty of the place.

We walked down the central corridor, past one of the more than 20 fireplaces, into a paneled reception room and down a circular staircase to "the pub."

Every square foot of Tyler Hall serves some function for the college. Even the pub, said to have been an authentic British tavern which was dismantled there and reassembled here, is used as a classroom.

Pausing in a long hallway, Sandra remembered more about her brushes with the energy in the old mansion.

"One of the things I had heard about others' experiences here is that when Stella lived here she would have elaborate dinners, and she would love to serve baked apples.

"That first night, I was here in this hallway and all of a sudden, out of nowhere, this total area filled up with the aroma of dinner and baked apples. It was midnight, and that was impossible, of course.

"It was her, welcoming me to her home.

"I was shocked. I said 'holy sugar!' Then, I said "hi, Stella!' I knew what was going on."

Sandra's stories did not center entirely on her first night as a security guard at BC3. As we stood at the doorway to the Music Room, she gathered her thoughts and in a hushed voice told of another night when she responded to an alarm which had tripped in that ornate room.

"I was coming into the Music Room," she said, "and had walked about halfway in and all of a sudden I heard a *swoosh*! Then, that curtain moved."

She pointed to one of several floor-to-ceiling curtains, maybe 15 feet long, which hung at windows which faced the state park land.

Sandra said after hearing the "swoosh" and seeing the curtain move she called for a backup security officer. She truly believed she had surprised an intruder and feared he or she may still be in the room or nearby.

When the other guard arrived they surveyed the room and the curtain "swooshed" again. The window was not open. There would have been no breeze to "swoosh" that curtain.

It should also be noted that the curtain in question shrouds a window which is high above a sheer cliff which drops down to the Neshaminy Creek. Only *Spiderman* could gain outside access to that window.

Sandra is not the only person at BC3 who has

reported ghostly activity. Some of that activity has taken place in The Orangery, where Stella tended her orange trees; and in the library auditorium.

But, it is in Tyler Hall where most of the ghost stories of BC3 take place. And, Sandra Sobek-Allen and others are convinced it is the gentle ghost of Stella Tyler who shakes things up once in a while in her old home.

"I'm very protective of Stella's spirit," Sandra said. "I heard a lot of positive things about her and feel that if Stella is in the building to protect it, it's my responsibility to protect Stella."

●

Broad Street, Quakertown, in an antique post card view. Note the name of the movie which was appearing at the time!

THE KISSING GHOST

Former Owner's Spirit Remains at Pineapple Hill B&B

Pineapple Hill Bed and Breakfast, between Washington Crossing and New Hope.

As it stands on a promontory along Route 32 between New Hope and Washington Crossing, the Pineapple Hill Bed & Breakfast offers an enviable location for visitors who come to Bucks County.

Close to the antique shops, historic sites, and cultural attractions of the region, the 1790-era manor house is set on about six acres between River Road and the canal. Its amenities include a comfortable common room, a hand-tiled pool, and five rooms and three suites furnished with original art and local antiques.

And, according to Kathryn and Charles Triolo, the innkeepers, Pineapple Hill also is home to at least two quite active ghosts.

"Many of our guests will attest to the presence of a resident ghost at the inn," the Triolos said in a prepared statement.

"The ghost is believed by some to be John Scott, who owned Pineapple Hill in the early 1800s. The ghost 'resides' in the oldest part of the house where Mr. Scott once lived...although he's been seen more than once in other parts of the house.

"While in bed at night, it's common to hear him creeping up the back stairs–only to feel him standing over your bed a few minutes later.

"One of the guests at Pineapple Hill even felt his lips graze her cheek!"

The prospect of a ghost in their tranquil inn doesn't

seem to bother the Triolos or their guests.

"Lights turning on and off by themselves, objects inexplicably moving, and mysterious breezes have also let us know that John Scott is with us," Mrs. Triolo continued.

And, they've even named one of their rooms the "John Scott Room."

But, John Scott may not be alone as a ghostly inhabitant of Pineapple Hill. Or perhaps, he receives an occasional visitor from the "other side."

"Guests have reported a nearly identical dream," the innkeeper said. "A man is riding on horseback. He's wearing black boots and a black wool coat adorned with gold buttons.

"The horse gallops down a tree-lined road. Suddenly, the horse stops and bucks fiercely. The man struggles to stay mounted. Dirt flies in the air as both horse and man cry out. The man struggles to regain control.

"Then, the guests wake up, never to find out what happened to the rider."

•

THE LIGHT-EATING GHOST

Strange Energies In New Hope's Gerenser Theater

The S.J. Gerenser Theater, New Hope.

We sat at a window table in the Logan Inn to speak not of the legendary ghosts of that New Hope landmark, but of the spirit forces that seem to swirl within the walls of the S.J. Gerenser Theater building at Bridge Street and Stockton Avenue.

Robert Gerenser hadn't had far to come for our rendezvous. His legendary Gerenser's Exotic Ice Cream shop and his Coryell's Ferry paddlewheel riverboat dock are just across South Main Street.

Gerenser is a native New Hoper. He's a borough councilman, a businessman, an actor, a local historian, and the man who portrayed Gen. George Washington in reenactments of Washington crossing the Delaware on

Christmas Day.

Bob is also the reluctant keeper of a ghost or two.

He takes a scientific approach to the supernatural. He needs proof. And, as a student of history he sets a high threshold of believability and demands certain levels of documentation.

But in one particular property his family has owned since the late 1960s, he and others have been so overwhelmed by the unexplainable that he finds it difficult to dismiss the incidents as mere happenstance or fate.

"I'm a generally optimistic person," he said. "I want to believe."

The S.J. Gerenser Theater is a landmark building which dates to the colonial era. Some space is leased to tenants, but Bob Gerenser stages special events and parties in the quaint auditorium.

For years, he has been vexed by a chilling chain of events which he first shrugged off as a series of practical jokes, pranks, or coincidences.

"It all came down to two or three categories," Bob finally reasoned. "Although I've had the electric service in that building redone from the ground up twice by now, I've continued to experience unusual electrical phenomena in the property.

"And, we talk about a 'tripping ghost,' or 'knocking-down ghost,' he continued. "And then there's our 'poltergeist thief ghost.'"

As Bob Gerenser–he of a calculating, pragmatic mind–speaks, it becomes more and more obvious that the energies at work in the old theater are edging him over the fence of believability.

That is especially evident when, with a dramatic flair, he draws a deep breath, plants his cup of hot cocoa firmly on a napkin, and speaks in hushed tones of the *dark entity* of the Gerenser Theater.

Dark, we soon learn, as in devoid of light.

"That building," he said, "in certain spots, *eats light*."

Pretty heady stuff from such a disciplined thinker. But he quickly explained.

"No matter how much light we bring into a situation, there are several spots in the building where you don't want to be.

"Your hair will stand up on the back of your neck. You will know something is wrong there."

During parties Bob has held in the theater, various electrical apparati have failed. On one occasion, a set of walkie-talkies and a remote control device gave out in one particular spot–a spot which was later read by a psychic as the spot where she felt the sad spirit of the victim of a suicide by hanging. That psychic, by the way, had no prior knowledge of the electronic anomalies.

As the man who stands at the bow of the boat

during the Washington's Crossing reenactments, and as a certified climber, Bob credits himself with an extraordinary sense of balance.

But his equilibrium is no match for what he calls the "tripping ghost." While he is quite adept and agile on ladders everywhere else, he is rendered embarrassingly klutzy by the unseen force in the theater.

"I've been picked up and thrown by that thing," he exclaimed.

Several tenants, including world-class athletes who train in a portion of the theater, have also reported losing their balance and feeling that there was really an invisible force at play.

Bob Gerenser, the historian, offered an almost whimsical possible explanation for the presence of the "tripping ghost."

In a search of past deeds and prior owners of the theater building, he noticed the name "Doan," as in the Doan Brothers. He did not suggest the actual Doan brothers ever owned the place, but did arch an eyebrow when he saw the a possible familial connection.

Abraham, Aaron, Mahlon, Levi, Joseph, and Moses Doan were notorious Tory outlaws whose misdeeds are part of Bucks County's folklore.

Bob joked that maybe they are the reason for his clumsiness.

"I would not be surprised," he mused with a wink

and a smirk, "that they've stayed behind and with their Tory leanings–they certainly know *my* politics–they want no part of me!"

Bob's flight of fancy ended with another sip of cocoa, another deep sigh, and an elaboration on the other spirits of the theater.

"Our real character, and this is one we feel very comfortable with, is someone we believe who just wants to be recognized.

"And, I'll go so as close to saying that this is a real paranormal phenomenon with a number of verifiable events that have happened associated with it," he continued in measured words.

It is what he calls the "poltergeist thief ghost."

It is what causes tools, jewels, all sorts of things to disappear at the most inopportune times and mysteriously reappear at the most inappropriate places. From garden shears to gold necklaces, many items belonging to many people over many years have been pilfered by the poltergeist.

"There is a presence at work there," Bob said as he teetered more precariously than ever from the credibility fence. "I liken it back to the forces allied against the *dark entity*."

One of the premiere events on the Gerenser Theater calendar is the invitation-only Colonial Christmas Ball. Bob remembered an incident at a recent

Ball which at once confounded and challenged him.

"When we do our Christmas Ball," he said, "it is extraordinarily authentic. Every hint of the 20th century is gone. We have acoustic music. Everyone is in authentic costumes. It is all candle-lit.

"When we shut down from this party, with 200 candles burning, a fire watch sits in the dark for 15 minutes after the candles have been extinguished.

"We wait...and we wait...and we wait. Then, we go around and inspect all the candles and sconces and chandeliers and table settings to make absolutely certain they are all extinguished.

"After being on this fire watch with three other very credible people, we went home. We came back the next morning to start to clean up, we walked in and one of the chandeliers on the stage was burning. No one else had been in there."

Bob has found a way to perhaps appease at least one of the spirits of the old theater.

"I send out close to 400 invitations to the Christmas Ball every year," he stated.

"The first name on the list is The Honorable Ghost. The address is that of the theater.

"Since inviting The Honorable Ghost, we are very confident that it is in attendance. And, we stopped having any difficulties."

•

THE GHOSTS OF THE BLACK BASS HOTEL

Several Spirits Stroll Through the Lumberville Landmark

The Black Bass Hotel, Lumberville.

When it was built in 1745 and for several years after, the Black Bass Hotel provided refuge from hostile natives.

When the Revolutionary War raged nearby, the Black Bass was well known as a bastion of loyalty to the Crown.

When the Delaware Canal was cut through what was the hotel's broad front lawn in 1832, the Black Bass became a popular place where canal-building laborers and then canal bargemen gathered.

And when President Grover Cleveland found out about the great fishing and incredible beauty up Lumberville way during his 1885-1889 term, he became a fairly regular guest at the hotel.

The Black Bass has had more than its share of history and mystery, and it is somehow appropriate that it has more than its share of ghosts.

"There are several ghosts here," longtime hostess Diane Robbins told us as we stood in the rustic "Lantern Room" of the inn.

That room itself harbors a ghost. Reported by several customers and staff members over the years, the Lantern Room ghost is described as a teary-eyed, elderly woman who stands forlorn and alone in a corner between the bar and a fireplace.

But it is on the second floor and in the canal-level tavern where most activity has been reported.

Although there have been no threatening incidents

at the Black Bass as the result of the spirits which roam its tight confines, the stories about the ghosts there are a bit alarming.

"One of our ghosts," Diane Robbins continued, "is a woman who has been seen floating through a door in one of our rooms. She carries a large, pearl-handled pistol."

The room is the Grover Cleveland Room.

In another room, named "Le Bastard," a sighting resulted in a delayed reaction by a guest, as Ms. Robbins remembered.

"A lady actually called me from England after she stayed here. About a week after she left, she called and asked me if there was anything she should have known about the inn. I asked her why. She told me that while she was lying in her bed, a green glow came from the center of the wall in her room.

"She looked out the window to see if it could possibly be a reflection of anything from across the river. Nothing was there, and nothing could explain that green glow."

Another ghost that has been reported on the second floor treads the uneven floors of the central hallway. She has been described as quite slender, dressed in a gauze gown, and seemingly lost in thought, trapped in time, or both.

Throughout the Black Bass are authentic antiques, a

pewter bar from Maxim's in Paris, countless artifacts which are loyal to the inn's Tory heritage, and several more ghosts.

For those, we venture to the canal and river level of the inn and into the main dining room.

Diners are given a sweeping view of the river and the Roebling-designed steel footbridge over it. They are given choices of fine selections from an extensive menu. And, they are given an opportunity to come face-to-face with a ghost.

Once a rough-and-tumble pub where canal builders and bargers tarried, the old cellar is now as charming as any dining room of any restaurant along River Road.

Tradition has it that in that old cellar, sometime in the late 1830s, a canal bargeman was either shot or stabbed to death during a brawl. Diane Robbins said his ghost has been seen there many times, but only by a select few.

"His ghost has been sighted by children. Only by children. No adults have ever seen this. Every time a child has described what they'd seen, they have given the very same, exact description–a bearded man, a big-brimmed hat with a plume, long hair, and knickers.

"He has been seen many times, but only by children."

Other reports of sightings of the bargeman's apparition dispute Diane's assertion. Several other

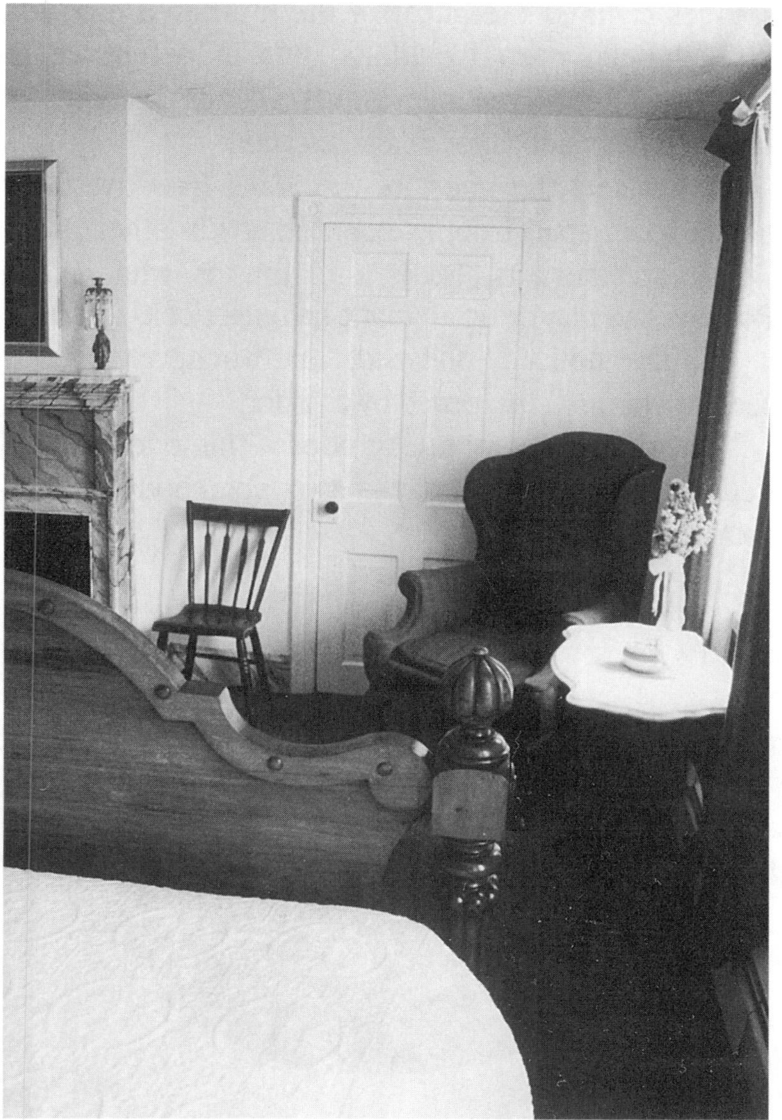

A pistol-packing ghost has walked through this door of the Grover Cleveland Room.

sources claimed the ghost of the murdered man has indeed been seen by adults, but–in deference to Diane–no first-hand eyewitness accounts could be obtained from adults for this publication.

What sets the ghost of the Black Bass riverfront tavern room apart from its counterparts in other Bucks County restaurants, B&Bs, and inns is what Diane Robbins says may be an aromatic harbinger of its arrival.

"I have noticed," she said, "that whenever anybody sees anything, it's preceded by an odor.

"It will be a very musty odor. This odor will be detected, and within a day or two, somebody will see something."

•

GHOSTS OF TOWNS AND COUNTRY

Ghost Stories Abound in Bucks County

There is scarcely one of the 610 square miles of Bucks County where a good ghost story or legend cannot be found.

From the bucolic north to the bustling south of the county, tales of intrigue and the unknown are very much a part of Bucks County's long and proud history.

In the following snapshots of haunted sites, we will hunt ghosts in covered bridges and modern fire halls. We will meet more of the characters who have come, gone, and sometimes remained behind in other forms. We will revisit places where ghosts once roamed–and perhaps still do.

An example of that latter category is a story once presented to those who patronized the **Doylestown Inn.**

In a newsletter published there in August, 1985, the editor cited several previous reports of ghosts in the building and added that many employees had "strange encounters" while on the job.

One night, several workers were winding up their shift when they clearly heard the sound of someone running up and down a staircase. When they investigated, they found no one.

On another occasion, a group of workers heard a

loud rattle of pots and pans coming from the kitchen. Again, when they checked, they were alone.

Still another employee, a bartender catching a nap in Room Two, was shaken awake. At precisely the moment he felt the shaking he heard a knock on the door of the room. He jumped out of bed to see who was there, and there was no one.

The inn was undergoing a sweeping renovation while this book was being prepared, and one worker on the site told us he had the constant feeling that an invisible entity was wandering through the project, keeping an eye on the workers and what would be its new home.

•

For generations, the **Harrow** was a landmark inn along the Durham Road at Routes 563 and 611. And, through at least two recent owners, its ancient (ca. 1744) frame provided some, er, harrowing experiences.

At the time of the publication of this book, the old inn was serving a different clientele. But when it was a public house, it generated a ghost story which is still told by folks like "Chef Tell" Erhardt, Klaus Reinecke, and Mark Healy.

Chef Tell once owned and lived in the Harrow. "The story that a number of people have told me," he remembered, "is that a woman threw her baby into a well there, and then dove in after her. Over the years I have heard many stories about people who say they have seen a woman carrying a baby in her arms, dressed in old-fashioned dress. I never experienced it or saw her, but many have."

Mark Healy, who also lived in the Harrow, heard the same story. "Apparently," he said, "that's an historical fact. But I don't know. The story is that from a third floor window, people would look down and see the woman carrying the baby."

Healy never saw anything either, but did admit that the place was, in his words, "spooky."

"On my first night there in the apartment," he said, "I was really spooked. It gets to you because it's a big, lonely building."

Klaus Reinecke owned the Harrow at that time, and through a German accent filtered through his 30 years in the United States, he assessed the stories he inherited when he bought the old inn.

"It seems like people are making things up," he said, "but they are not. These things really do exist.

"There are good ghosts and bad ghosts. If you leave them alone, and they are comfortable with you, they leave *you* alone."

•

We leave the inns, B&Bs and restaurants of Bucks County for a few moments now and venture into some locations where ghosts have etched their presences.

Based on long-standing rumors of a haunting there, members of the Philadelphia Ghost Hunters Alliance took their equipment and there sense of adventure to the **Trevose Firehouse** and **Twining Hall** along Street Road in Trevose.

The group had been informed that the baseline of the haunting was the fact that Twining Hall, a banquet hall adjacent to the actual fire station, was built on what was a graveyard. Volunteer firefighters and patrons of the banquet hall have reported sightings over the past several years.

There, they experienced several disturbances which ranged from a constant uneasy feeling to a jiggling door knob to dark figures behind the ballroom bar to an actual apparition of what was described as a "man in old clothing" in the kitchen of the banquet hall.

In his report, PGHA president Lewis Gerew mentioned four incidents which caused him to conclude that "there very well may be some spirit activity here.

Another member of the investigative team was quite a bit more convinced. "There is *definitely* haunting activity here," he wrote in his summary.

•

As this book was being researched, the tedious job of moving a large antiques and furniture shop was underway. The shop was forced to relocate from the old farm property in **Holicong**, and as it moved, those who worked there distanced themselves from some very eerie occurrences.

We are not at liberty to pinpoint the property, but those who once toiled at the sprawling shop can say that they believe the place is haunted.

Furniture preparer Tom Bintoiff decided to wrap things up for the night when he and a co-worker were startled. "Something came down the hall," he said. "It wasn't something we saw clearly. But it came down with a swoosh, if you know what I mean. Hell, I scurried out of the place!

"Both of us agreed it was some kind of presence. It wasn't the wind. It was fast. It was cold. It moved the chandeliers that were hanging there."

Another employee said he was in a particular corner on the second floor when something grabbed his arm. Then, he felt as if his shirt had caught on a nail. He spun around. No one was there, and his shirt was pulled from his pants and standing out in mid-air.

Dark shadows and silhouettes, the faint sound of a name–*Carmella*–being called out, and the sound of footsteps creaking up a staircase made just about everybody who worked at the antiques shop on Route 202 believe that they were never really alone in their old quarters.

•

One of the loveliest of all the lovely inns around

Bucks County is **Evermay on-the-Delaware**, near Erwinna.

Built in the 18th century, extensively remodeled and enlarged in 1871 and listed on the National Register of Historic Places, the retreat is set on 25 impeccable acres.

As we prowled the depth and breadth of Bucks County in search of ghost stories, we stopped at the country house hotel which is said to have been a favorite country retreat of the Barrymore family.

Dawn Smigo, innkeeper, has heard several stories about the history of the property and its relationship to things ghostly.

"Often times," she said, "in the Erwin Room on the second floor, people claim there is some sort of presence."

That chamber, formally known as The Col. William Erwin Room, is in the original Federal-style section of the house.

Guests and housekeepers have reported creepy, but comfortable feelings in another room–The Chief Nutimus Loft,

Named after the native chief and medicine man who, with his colleague Tishekunk, met nearby with John and Thomas Penn to examine treaties between the English and Indians, the loft is situated just under the eaves on the inn's fourth floor.

"People think there's a very strong presence up there," Ms. Smigo added.

In the course of researching another ghost story in New Hope, we came across another ghost story about Evermay.

We dropped by the Three Cranes Gallery on South Main Street with questions about that place when a clerk there told us he had a personal experience not at Three Cranes, but farther up the river.

That experience was at what is now Evermay. That clerk was Harry Matthews, who grew up just down the road from Evermay.

"At the time," Harry said, "there was just an eccentric old man living there. He let some friends of mine and me inside and we wandered around.

"We went down to the basement. We were behind some wall down there and I came around the corner and saw some type of ghostly apparition go right through a wall, through a room, and into another wall.

"There were no sounds, nothing at all. There was no definition to it, just a cloud-like vision."

Harry had heard, as had Dawn Smigo, that on the property–perhaps under the mansion–was an Indian burial ground.

No matter what, neither Dawn, nor any guests at Evermay, nor Harry Matthews has ever felt anything intimidating or threatening by the almost everpresent

EverMay on-the-Delaware.

"presences" and "visions" of Evermay.

As Harry said, "I wasn't frightened at all then, and I remember it like it was yesterday.

"It's something I will never forget."

•

The **Richlandtown Inn**, on South Main Street in the town from which it got its name, already had a fine reputation as a popular restaurant in upper Bucks County when Hans and Bonnie Paulsen took the place over in 1983.

And, as they were soon to discover, it also had a reputation of being haunted.

Opened in 1812 as the Spread Eagle Hotel, the building features a 35-foot oak bar brought from Allentown by horse and wagon by John Hinkle in 1904.

The Paulsens operated what they called the Richlandtown Hotel until they sold it to Jane Watson Gimpel in 1993. Gimpel made several improvements and renamed it as an "Inn."

Ms. Gimpel has not had any personal contact with the spirits in her inn, but does not reject the stories told by the Paulsens and others.

Through the years, guest reported doors opening with no human aid, shoes and other personal items moving on their own, lights and radios switching on or off, and other assorted mischievous and baffling events.

"We had about five different incidents," Bonnie

Paulsen told us. "One, a waitress of ours whose brother died a week before was in the middle dining room doing afternoon cleanup. All of a sudden she went *'AAH!'* and I went in to see what was the matter.

"Her hair was standing on end. She said that a rush of cold air came by her body. And when she cleaned the table off, her brother's name was written on the placemat and the placemat had been turned upside down!"

Visibly shaken by the memory, Bonnie continued.

"That same day was when I got involved. I hadn't believed much, but I happened to be sitting with a customer who used to pepper his soup to death every lunch time.

"We were sitting there talking and that same waitress came to fill up the salts and peppers and that pepper shaker the guy had been using was missing.

"Now, I know he had just used that pepper shaker. His soup was black on top as usual. So, I'm teasing him. I said, get up, we're going to frisk you–just teasing him."

Bonnie remembered one Sunday morning when she came into that same room and noticed that everything–everything–in the room was cocked slightly to the right. "I mean everything, she said. "The fire extinguisher, a picture on the wall, a chair, everything was shifted just to the right. There was no explanation to that," she shrugged.

•

This probably won't come as a surprise to you, but when Washington crossed the Delaware, he did not do so at the village of Washington Crossing.

That name didn't come along until the Commonwealth of Pennsylvania bought up most of what was Taylorsville and changed the name to honor and identify the place where Washington's troops crossed the Delaware to attack Trenton.

In the thick of the historic village is the **Washington Crossing Inn**.

Built as a house by Bernard Taylor in 1812, what is now a fine dining establishment also holds within it a ghost.

"Up in the attic," innkeeper Frank Cipullo said, "the lights go on and off. The shades are drawn when they shouldn't be. Sometimes we get some spooky breezes up there."

Cipullo added that several past and present employees have reported seeing and hearing strange sights and sounds.

He is also fairly convinced that he knows whose spirit is locked inside the inn.

"It's Bernard Taylor," he said. "He's still living in the inn. He's a permanent guest!"

•

Just north of Lake Nockamixon in the hamlet of Strawntown is the old stagecoach stop once known as the Long House Tavern and later called the Stage Coach Inn.

It is now The **Raven's Nest Inn**. Ah, The Raven! Once upon a midday dreary we stopped by the roadside inn to search for the origin of its ominous name.

Did flocks of ravens infest the property? Was the innkeeper a Poe aficionado?

No–Al and Rena Pray named it after their oldest daughter, Raven. The "nest" was added because the place was to be Raven's nest egg for college tuition. No Poe, nevermore.

Al and Raven Pray both agree there is a definite presence that permeates the 1746-era building. They do know that a former owner died there and they say it is his ghost, just keeping watch. "It's as if somebody is always watching over my shoulder," Al said. "It's scary here late at night."

One late night, Al remembered, he and a regular patron were sitting at one end of the bar talking. The place was closed and they were the only ones in the barroom.

They both were startled when an empty beer bottle standing on the other end of the bar tipped over and rolled toward them.

There is also a persistent rumor that the notorious Doan (a.k.a. Doane) Brothers and/or other members of their Tory gang of outlaws stashed some of their ill-

The Raven's Nest.

begotten plunder in an old well which is under a cement slab on the Raven's Nest property.

Al Pray once tried to find the loot, but had no success.

•

Among the dozen covered bridges still standing in Bucks County, the Beaver Dam, or **Van Sant Bridge** is the one which has drawn the attention of ghost hunters from miles around.

The 86-feet long, 15-feet wide bridge was built in 1875 over the Pidcock Creek. Because of its proximity to New Hope and Washington Crossing, it is one of the most traversed covered bridges in the county.

And, it is said to be the most haunted.

There are legends galore about the old bridge. One has horse thieves being hanged from its rafters. Another claims that a woman murdered her baby inside the darkened passageway.

The ghosts of the Van Sant Bridge were mentioned in documents dating as far back as 1869 when what was described as yellow in color followed a young man from a nearby woods and into the bridge.

A group of ghost hunters from New Jersey probed the bridge just prior to publication of this book and claimed to have seen the spirit of a man sitting on the stone wall which leads into the bridge. They also detected a shadowy form which seemed to glide through the Van Sant.

Another would-be ghost hunter told us she and several others once went to the bridge to see what they could see and hear what they could hear.

What they claimed to have seen was a glowing form which materialized as if from nowhere inside the bridge. What they claimed to have heard was the muffled scream of a young woman and the garbled crying of a young child.

•

Throughout Bucks County there are countless private residences where ghosts roam free. And throughout the years several homeowners have gone public with their hauntings.

A home on Trenton Avenue in Fallsington drew much attention in the 1970s with its Hessian ghosts, and the experiences of a household in Langhorne received press coverage at about the same time.

And, it was in the early 1970s when Arthur Moeller, who at this writing was manager of Nockamixon State Park, was manager of Independence Hall in Philadelphia when it was a state-run facility.

Moeller came up empty when we asked him about any ghosts which may prowl the grounds of Nockamixon. But, he did relate a story which has stuck with him since he resided in the **Dunk's Ferry** house at Neshaminy State Park during his term as

Independence Hall manager.

"I was newly married and my wife and I lived there by ourselves in the early 1970s," he said.

"We were in bed one night in the summertime. We had the fan running and the windows open," he continued.

That warm, quiet night was suddenly interrupted by a sound which rattled both of them.

"We heard footsteps above us," Moeller said with a tinge of nervousness in his voice.

"The steps came from up in the attic. They went from one end of the attic, the length of the house, to the other end. So, I got out of bed and got my shotgun and my dog. I opened the door to go up in the attic.

"I tried to get the dog to go up first," he kidded. "I pushed him up from behind. He didn't want to go. So, I went up.

"I only got my head above the floor level and I looked around. I didn't see anything."

Scanning the empty space, Moeller was satisfied that no *visible* intruder was present.

"That dog never really did go up there," he continued. "So I came back down and got back into bed."

Relieved, Moeller returned to the business of the moment–trying to get back to sleep.

"And then," he recalled, "we heard the footsteps

again!"

He figured that there was no point in going back upstairs. There was nothing, no one, there.

Or was there?

Moeller hadn't heard any stories about any hauntings in the old Dunk's Ferry House. An experienced park ranger, he knew and knows the difference between rummaging rodents, scrambling squirrels, and the like.

"No," he assured us, "what I heard were *footsteps!*"

•

Unexplained phenomena experienced in youth often–no pun intended–haunt people the rest of their lives.

So it is with a woman who spent the first half of her life in a home along New Road in Upper Southampton Township.

"I was 18 years old at the time," she said, "and after it happened I figured that people would think I was crazy if I told them."

Her family's home was built in the 1940s, and she had been told by a very reliable source that a previous resident had died there and after his cremation his ashes were scattered in the back yard.

That, she believes, was the baseline for a strange series of events.

"One summer night I got home and the back door

was open. No lights were lit inside the house," she remembered. She summoned a neighbor who cautiously entered the house and the two of them found nothing awry. Still, she could never figure out how the lights–which she remembered turning *on*–turned *off,* and how the door came to be open.

"So," she continued, "the next time I went out I made absolutely sure I left the lights on before I left. When I came home, the lights were off. That really got me wondering."

Throughout her late teens, some of them spent working at the nearby Johnsville Naval Air Development Center, the woman was vexed by various events.

Once, she was startled to enter a room and see two rather large wall hangings propped neatly on the floor against the wall upon which they had hung. It was as if someone–and no one ever admitted doing so–had carefully removed them from the wall and placed them on the floor.

The woman eventually married and moved from her parents' home on New Road. Soon after, she got a phone call.

"My mom called and said that she had heard a large boom, and thought at first it was a truck passing by. She looked out the back door, where my father would pull his car in, and where his car would normally be, she saw the face of the man whose ashes had been strewn in the yard. She was really shaken up."

On another occasion, the woman called home and was herself shaken by the answer.

"It sounded like someone picked up the receiver, so I said 'hello,' but nobody answered. I said 'hello' a few more times and nobody answered, and nobody hung up.

"Finally, I just hung up the phone and went about my business. I called my mom later in the day and told her about it. I said that dad must have answered the phone this morning and must have been half asleep because he picked up the phone and didn't answer me.

"She told me that he wasn't home at the time. He had gotten up early to go to work. Then, she said she had been at church and wondered why the phone was off the hook.

"I thought that was interesting," she added.

Eventually, the young woman (who asked to remain anonymous) discovered that her father had been keeping a secret.

"He was your typical 'John Wayne' kind of guy," she said. "But later, after all this had happened to my mother and me, he told us that when we first moved in he though he would hear footsteps upstairs. He'd go up to check, but nobody was ever there.

"For him to say that was quite amazing."

•

Laura remembers it as if it was yesterday. It was an event so bizarre that she could never forget it. And, as you read this account, you may question its validity and, perhaps, Laura's veracity.

But be assured that the middle-aged professional woman (who, at this writing, was director of a teen drug and alcohol prevention program) has questioned the event many, many times since it took place starting October 6, 1984 in a comfortable Colonial home on Franklin Street in Morrisville.

She remembers the date well as it was the date of her wedding.

The story began when a stranger entered the reception hall and presented her with a congratulatory Mylar balloon. From that moment, her life and her belief in whatever lies beyond life was forever altered.

"This very tall man, about six-five, walked into the wedding reception with a bottle of champagne and a Mylar balloon attached to it," Laura (not her real name) remembered.

"We took the balloon home. You know that they last quite a while. Well, two days later we noticed that the balloon started following me around. At first we figured it was an air draft, static electricity, or something.

"But, if I went down stairs in the morning, it would come down the stairs and just kind of hang out in the room I was in. It would come up at night and hover around the bed.

"This went on for about a week or so, and it would really spook us out."

Several friends and relatives attest to the bouncing, stalking balloon. It had been sent to the newlyweds by a friend and the tall stranger was a delivery man for a local shop. In the first few weeks, the balloon which followed Laura like a shadow was nothing more than an unnerving curiosity.

Laura said the house seemed to have its own unexplainable quirks which were (probably) not related to the balloon incident.

She and her husband often heard what sounded like chairs being moved on a floor above them. They heard footsteps. But the balloon's behavior defied all reason. And one night, something so incredible happened that to this day it confounds the woman who has since moved from that Morrisville home.

One night as her husband was working late, Laura was alone in the bedroom. It was around 11 p.m., and the balloon was in position.

"The balloon came to the foot of the bed and started bobbing up and down and up and down. Now, that *really* spooked me," she continued.

"I got on the phone, called my husband and asked when he was coming home from work. He said he'd be home shortly. So, I just sat there.

"Then, all of a sudden there was a tapping. It sounded like it was coming from the headboard of the bed. It tapped out a rhythm–a pattern."

Laura took mental note of that pattern. Confused and frightened, she called her husband again and related the "rhythm" to him.

He and she could never have imagined what was to follow.

"It turned out," Laura said with a tinge of nervousness creeping into her voice, "that it was the Morse Code for the ham radio signal of one of my husband's buddies who had died just before our wedding!"

Upon hearing that Laura held the phone, frozen in fear and disbelief.

The story is not over.

When her husband told her his deceased friend's name, Laura repeated it aloud, alone in that room.

"And at the moment I called out my husband's dead buddy's name," she said, "the balloon went down to the floor. And that was it."

The balloon simply dropped, never to follow her again–except in her memory.

•

As we gathered information for this book, a good chunk of time and a large percentage of interviews were cast aside when the property owners declined to have their personal or property identities made public.

This, of course, we understand and respect.

Carolyn Hughes, who owns and resides on the **Spotted Cow Farm** near Ottsville, had no problem sharing her story. She said it might be the best thing she could do for her invisible, mischievous housemate.

The innkeeper of the apparently ghost-free Bridgeton Inn, Hughes said her house on Geigel Hill was built in the early 1800s, and had been the centerpiece of a working dairy farm.

Quite proud of the lovely property, Carolyn is also quite protective of her resident wraith.

"She's female and she's *very* benevolent," Carolyn said. "She does strange things like move plants around, or if I've made a change in the arrangement where I have my plants she'll move them to a different place.

"She also makes a lot of noise at night.

"When I first moved in there, I thought it was the cat. Somebody was knocking things down in the kitchen and the kitchen is up the curved stairs down from my bedroom. I kept hearing things. I would go down and check and I'd see nothing. But things were in disarray.

"She apparently likes to cook because it was always pots and pans and things making the noise. But generally speaking, sometimes we just have a presence. We don't know. She will just make the lights flicker all the time."

Nearly everyone in Carolyn Hughes extended family has been introduced to and believes in the ghost, whoever it may be.

"I haven't named here yet," Carolyn continued. "I haven't got a feel for it. I keep thinking I'm going to get a sign as to who she is.

"I'm sure her genesis is from the 1700s or 1800s. I think she is a woman between 20 and 30 years old. She's kind of frivolous. She's not very grounded, as far as I can tell. She must be creative, though, because she does creative things.

"She'll take all of my knitting and the balls will be out of the basket. I have a big place where I sit in the cabin. And, I have a huge basket of knitting there. I knit several projects at the same time, and many times, all the balls are mixed up.

"Of course, I blame it on the cat, but the cat never goes near there.

"I think my ghost was a young wife. I've asked her to leave me a sign, but she hasn't revealed herself to that degree."

Again, Carolyn Hughes was quite content to share her story with our readers.

"Oh," she said, "I think she'd be very proud of this. I think she does very mischievous things because she wants to be recognized, wants to be noticed.

"I have the feeling that the people who lived here

before probably didn't pay much attention to her because they were gone all the time and they had teenage girls who were very noisy.

"So, I think she was quiet for a good while. When I moved in, she pretty much had the run of the house."

•

By his own admission, Richard Butkus is "gregarious." That would ensure that a stay at the **Hollileif Bed and Breakfast** on the Durham Road (Route 413) in Wrightstown will be filled with clever banter and ebullience.

Perhaps some of Richard's conversation may even spill over into the supernatural.

Richard and Ellen Butkus have never seen anything themselves, but several of their best guests have had encounters in the 18th century farmhouse rooms–some encounters this "family" publication cannot fully address.

The couple purchased the Hollileif ("We inherited the name," Ellen said. "The 'holli' part is because of the holly tree out front and the 'leif,' we were told, means 'beloved' in Norwegian.") in 1990 and were told by the previous owners that with the B&B came a *boo* or two. Ghosts, that is.

It's interesting to note that Richard Butkus is an accomplished dowser. And, at the drop of a hat, he'll instruct anyone who asks in the fine art of using a divining rod.

It was a dowser who also used his skills to identify some of the energy within the walls of the beautifully-decorated fieldstone home and on the more than five acres of grounds.

Richard said that although he's never witnessed an apparition in the Hollileif, he has often heard something.

"I'll be by myself in the living room and I'll hear floorboards squeaking in the upstairs hallway when there's nobody up there. At first I disregarded it, but then I started paying attention and it made me wonder."

Those former owners told the Butkuses that a guest there had told them that they saw a filmy form of a long-haired woman in Room Four.

Strange things have happened in that same room and at least two others.

Ellen remembered a couple who spent their wedding night and then their fifth anniversary night in the Hollileif. When they checked out the second time the woman told Ellen that she had witnessed the rocking chair in the room rocking gently back and forth in the middle of the night while her husband was sound asleep next to her.

Another woman once reported seeing a misty figure gravitate down the central hallway. As she stared, the figure compressed and slid under the door of Room Three.

And Room One was the scene of a most bizarre encounter which was reported by a male guest.

He told the innkeepers that sometime during the night a female ghost came through the door–*through* the door, that is, and sidled up to the bed. Then, it sidled up to him *in* the bed and, well...we'll leave it there.

Should you drop by the Hollileif, maybe the "gregarious" Richard will finish the story for you.

•

If there is any doubt in your mind that we did not go to every corner of Bucks County in our exhaustive research for this book, we submit the following story from just about as far north in the county as one may venture.

The **Riegelsville Inn** was built in 1838 by Benjamin Reigel, for whom the "ville" is known.

And, proprietor Betty Giddio said that although the ghost story of her historic property is a bit nebulous, it nonetheless gives the place character.

"There was a young woman," she said, "who used to stay here, up on the third floor. She told us she would hear unexplained sounds and really believed that there was someone–a spirit–who walked around up there."

Betty has never seen anything in her charming inn, but does not rule out the possibility that does have a rather permanent guest.

THE BEARDED GHOST OF COLVIN'S FERRY

Does a Shaggy Spirit Still Haunt the Riverbanks of Morrisville?

The site of Colvin's Ferry, Morrisville.

·BUCKS COUNTY GHOST STORIES·

There are times when the pursuit of ghost stories takes odd twists and turns into the most unexpected places and times.

Take, for example, the story of a rather frightening specter who haunted a house in Morrisville more than a century ago.

It was in an old scrapbook in the dusty archives of the Historical Society of Pennsylvania that a clipping emerged with the headline, *An Unshaven Ghost: He Has a Black Beard and Goes to a Party*.

The story appeared in no less a believable broadsheet than *The New York Times* of Sunday, February 27, 1887.

The headline caught our attention. We were researching information for our 1998 book, *Philadelphia Ghost Stories*. And as tempting as this headline was, we shunted it aside as it was about the ghostly goings-on in a place far up the Delaware River from Philadelphia–Morrisville, Pa.

Still, we filed the story for future reference and inclusion in any book on Bucks County we might someday compile.

The future is now.

The place was, as the story noted, "a quaint old ferry house on the banks of the Delaware opposite Trenton."

The place is now Morrisville.

So, to the Morrisville Free Library we went, seeking

more information about this old ferry, and perhaps that old ghost story.

The ghost story had apparently been lost in time. But information about the ferry was abundant.

It was best known historically as "Colvin's Ferry," but was operated from 1772-1792 by Patrick Colvin as the "Blazing Star."

It was noted by historian James E. Wood that "when Washington retreated across New Jersey, he crossed the Delaware at Colvin's Ferry." It was, of course, not *the* "Washington Crossing the Delaware" episode of American history. *That* took place up river a bit.

Other references to the old ferry house claim that indeed, Washington was entertained at Colvin's place during the crossing. Further, financier Robert Morris (from whom the town got its name) is said to have resided there after the Revolutionary War, and the ferry house was later occupied by the French Gen. Victor Jean Maria Moreau.

The house apparently met its fate when the present railroad bridge was erected. Any trace of the old ferry house vanished in the early part of the 20th century.

But oh, what tales those walls could have told!

And one of those tales would have been a good, old fashioned ghost story.

The year was 1887, and the teller of the tale was John Peze, who had just moved into the old ferry house in January of that year.

Peze, described as a "gray-whiskered carter," had occupied the place with his wife and several members of his extended family.

The *Times* writer set an eerie stage for the ghostly encounter. The words warrant remembering:

It was the dead of night and the cold moon was giving a faint and melancholy glance into the apartment when (Peze) heard the door opening and the wind breathe through the back casements.

When in...walked a ghost!

As the uninvited visitor made its way into Peze's bedchamber, it wheezed and moaned. As if those sounds weren't enough to send chills down John Peze's spine, he sat up in his bed only to see the cloudy, faint figure of a rather unkempt man standing in his doorway.

A thick, matted, black beard covered the spirit's chin and equally ragged, long hair drooped from his head. He wore a white undershirt and black pants. Peze said he believed there was blood oozing from an open wound in the apparition's neck.

After his initial fear and shock subsided, Peze rose from his bed to see if this was man or phantom who had come to call.

As he cautiously approached the figure, he readily determined it was not of his time and place. It was, he knew all to well, a ghost.

That bearded spirit backed away from John Peze as he walked toward him. Slowly, with sorrowful moans echoing softly, the ghost glided through corridors and down stairs with Peze in curious pursuit.

Upon reaching the cellar of the old ferry house, the ghost vanished into thin air.

John Peze doubtlessly returned to his bedroom, but whether he slept any more that night is a matter for speculation.

Other members of his family were introduced to this unearthly intruder a few nights later when the image appeared to them and a group of visiting friends.

And still once more, the ghost appeared to Mrs. Peze, who fainted at the sight of the fierce-looking wraith.

As Peze, his family members, and neighbors wrestled with the notion of a ghost in the old Colvin's Ferry house, they tried to find a possible source of the haunting.

Some folks in the area recalled a death that took place in the house some 30 years before Peze's sighting. And others dismissed the entire incident as the product of overactive imaginations.

Peze, in turn, dismissed those thoughts. He knew what he saw, knew it was not of this world or of his imagination, and stood by his story. As did the others who saw the bloody, bearded ghost of Colvin's Ferry.

There is little to remind anyone today of what was a very important ferry crossing at what is now the area around "Welcome Park" along the Delaware River at Green Street.

These days, a railroad bridge vaults overhead, the Trenton skyline looms to the east, and the riverbank is littered with discarded tires and assorted rummage down where, so long ago, that bloody, bearded ghost is said to have strolled.

Perhaps that ghost strolls there still today.

•

Welcome to Room Six at the Logan Inn, New Hope.

ROOM SIX

The Ghosts of New Hope's Legendary Logan Inn

The Logan Inn, New Hope.

You won't find ghosts among the offerings of the Logan Inn. You will find sixteen guest rooms furnished in colonial style, the formal Gallery Room or glass-enclosed Garden Dining Rooms, and a comfortable tavern where locals cross paths with visitors from around the world.

But nowhere in the brochures or advertisements for what is one of the five oldest continuously-operated inns in the United States will you find any mention of any ghosts.

The Logan Inn was built around 1722 by the founder of New Hope, John Wells. He called it the Ferry Tavern and the town was called Wells Ferry.

As Wells Ferry became New Hope, the Ferry Tavern became the Logan Inn.

The town's name changed when Benjamin Parry rebuilt his fire-ravaged flour mills and called them the "New Hope Mills."

The Logan was named after both a Lenni-Lenape chief and William Penn's secretary.

If that is a bit confusing to you, you join a club which is nearly three centuries old.

Native chief Wingohocking spent much time in conference with Penn's trusted aide James Logan. Through various negotiations and parlays, the chief became so enamored with the colonial secretary that he paid the highest tribute he could by "trading names" with the settler. Thus, Wingohocking became Logan. Logan became Wingohocking.

But Wingohocking, the colonial aid, knew that his new name wouldn't fare well in his social circles. He accepted the tribute in friendship but dropped it and assigned the name to a local creek. Logan remained Logan. As did Wingohocking.

In about 1828, a ten-foot metal figure which represented Chief Wingohocking, er, Chief *Logan* was erected on the tavern property and the place became known as the Logan House. A modern interpretation of the reclining, pipe-smoking chief still adorns the inn's sign.

Listed on the National Register of Historic Places, the Logan Inn has long been a crossroads of social, business, and, as you will soon learn, supernatural activity in New Hope.

Oscar Hammerstein II, the Marx Brothers, most of those who made up the Algonquin Hotel "Round Table" (Dorothy Parker, George S. Kaufman, Moss Hart, et al), and other luminaries passed through or stayed at the Logan.

As New Hope grew as a center for arts and theater, the Logan Inn grew in stature. And through it all, its owners preserved the simple dignity of a small-town hostelry.

The Logan was last renovated thoroughly ($1.6

million's worth of thoroughness) in 1987.

It was just after that project when Gwen Davis became innkeeper of the legendary inn.

And now, the ghosts.

For decades, the Logan Inn has been reputed to be haunted. Some psychics and mediums have proclaimed it to be one of the most authentically haunted buildings in America.

Some say it's haunted by the ghost of an anonymous little boy. Some say Aaron Burr's spirit rambles within the Logan. Some have seen a fully-uniformed Revolutionary War-era soldier walk silently from the kitchen into the tavern.

Several previous owners and current employees have reported a shadowy figure pass through the walls of the tavern or glide by the Ferry Street windows. And, one individual swears that he has seen the fireplace ignite into full flame all by itself.

The stories are plentiful, and most quite believable. But if anyone holds within them the chronicles of the odd and unexplained of the Logan Inn, it is Gwen Davis.

Very interested and involved in area historical organizations and activities, Gwen does not take reports of ghosts lightly. But the evidence of the haunting of the Logan Inn is overwhelming.

And much of that evidence has come from a room in the southeastern corner of the second floor.

Room Six.

"I find the oddest thing about that room," Gwen said, "is that's it's always the coldest room in the house. At that location, it shouldn't be."

The room, with windows on both walls, gets the sunlight first and longest of all rooms. Still, there is a definite chill throughout the room, throughout the hours and seasons.

And, the tales of strange encounters and activity in Room Six have come from a broad spectrum of the inn's clientele and staff.

"People have been tapped on their shoulder and no one was there," Ms. Davis continued. "I recently had a man stay in Room Six. He came down to the desk and told me the weirdest thing had happened to him. In the middle of the night, someone opened the door–the door that was double-locked. He got up, looked out in the hallway, and there was nobody there.

"He told me other things that had happened, but wouldn't elaborate," she added. What's more, he told Gwen that he was in town, in the Logan, researching ghost stories.

"He said that of all the places in the world he had stayed, this is where he had the most unusual experiences."

Other guests have said that while the spirit which seems to reside in Room Six means no harm, it can be vexing. On one occasion, a woman reported that her pillow was pulled from under her head in the middle of the night. Several people say the saw the silhouette of a woman standing inside the door.

One individual took a photograph of a ten-foot high portrait of Charles and Elizabeth Lutz, the grandparents of a former owner of the inn. The painting was positioned prominently at the top of the stairs which lead to the guest rooms.

After the photo was processed, Gwen received a telephone call from the guest, who told her that in the picture, between Charles and Elizabeth, was the distinct image of a man with long hair, dressed in a cloak.

In the painting, it is obvious that Charles has a sprig of lavender in his lapel and Elizabeth has lavender in her hair. The aroma of lavender has often been detected in Room Six.

And, at least one person told Gwen that the spirit in Room Six is Emily Hirtreiter Lutz, the daughter-in-law of the Lutzes and mother of the former innkeeper. Emily did pass away in the Logan Inn.

With the steady stream of stories regarding the energies which remain in the Logan, does Gwen Davis believe the inn is truly haunted by ghosts?

"Oh yes, definitely," she said, without hesitation. "And the one that I find very eerie is in the basement.

"During the Revolutionary War, troops would march

Some believe "Emily" is among the ghosts of the Logan Inn.

from Valley Forge to New Hope. It took them about four days to get here and three days to cross the river. There were a lot of deaths that occurred due to the weather.

"They would store the bodies in the kitchen basement because the ground was too frozen to bury them outside.

"There is a story–which I don't think is true–that they were cremated, but one wasn't *totally* cremated. It's his ghost which remains down there."

As the one who can usually be found at the tiny desk in the tight "lobby" of the inn, Gwen has become a funnel through which guest after guest and employee after employee have told their ghostly tales.

"We had a former head of housekeeping here who was working with another man and in the middle of the night, about three or four in the morning, each one thought the other one was walking in the hallways of different floors," she said. The two men eventually caught up to each other and realized that neither was ever where the other thought they had been.

Trish Gazzillo has been head of housekeeping at the Logan Inn since just after the last major renovation. "I've had a couple of weird things happen," she said.

"I've seen shadows in a couple of the rooms. I've heard my name called out, and I've come down and asked Gwen if she'd called me and she told me she hadn't."

Trish also often bears the brunt of guests who either embrace or renounce their brushes with the paranormal. Most vivid in her mind is the report from one couple who said they distinctly heard the sound of a baby crying in the bathroom of...Room Six.

"I don't believe in any of it myself," Trish said. "It's just that when something does happen to *me*, it makes me think that maybe it *is* true."

The Logan Inn serves as the starting point of very popular ghost walking tours of New Hope, and has been investigated by nearly everyone who seriously studies the supernatural.

And yet, the Logan Inn does not promote its ghosts. Gwen understands the sensitivities of some guests. "If they ask, we'll tell them," she said.

Sometimes, they don't have to be told. They find out for themselves. And usually, they accept their unseen (most of the time) companions.

"No one has ever told us it's an unfriendly spirit," Ms. Davis said.

•

GHOST TOWN

Ghosts Are a Fact of Life in New Hope

Bert Johnson, businessman and borough councilman in New Hope when this book was written, told us that if we were looking for ghosts and ghost stories, we were in the right place.

He quipped that if we walked the streets long enough and knocked on enough doors, we would find that every third building in New Hope was haunted.

We didn't have enough time or energy to take on his challenge. But, we defer to his wisdom.

As we asked shop owners and citizens of New Hope about ghosts, we were told of a spirit that rocks away on a rocking chair in the Inn at Phillips Mill, artist Joseph Pickett's ghost in his old home, and stories of phantom hitchhikers, screaming babies, and the "woman in white" who walks through the town from time to time.

Every year, thousands of people come to New Hope to stroll its streets not only in search of good theater, food, art, shopping, and culture. Many come to take the excellent ghost tours, hear the ghost stories and see the haunted places.

Owner of the Three Cranes Gallery, Bert Johnson was introduced to the ghosts of the town early on.

"When I first moved to New Hope," he said, I had a shop on Mechanic Street. I had heard a lot of stories about ghosts on that street. I had someone employed by me who had left his jacket in the shop after we had closed.

"I pulled up to the curb so he could let himself back in the shop to get his jacket. He yelled from the door that he saw a man in the shop.

"He went in to see who it was, but didn't find anyone. He described the man as if he was wearing a military jacket with epaulets and brass buttons.

"When I talked to people later, I found that there were stories of a soldier's ghost in the building."

Bert was quickly introduced to the ghosts of New Hope.

In what is now La Terrazza, a pleasant Italian restaurant along the towpath of the canal, Bert swore he witnessed a woman in a black dress wander into the kitchen. While he swore in the instant that what he saw was a flesh-and-blood woman, he questioned that supposition after learning that the restaurant, once called the Towpath House, was haunted by a woman in black.

La Terrazza is in a cluster of three buildings on Mechanic Street at the canal. Their collective address is 18-20 Mechanic Street, and their owner is Paul Licitra.

Licitra, who was also executive director of the New Hope Arts Commission at the time this book was written, is a sensitive, spiritual man who is very aware and sometimes appreciative of the energies he is certain remain earthbound after death.

He lives in the former residence of an artist whose work is almost certainly in your home–perhaps in your pocket–as you read this.

Dr. Selma H. Burke was a world-class painter and sculptor. Born in North Carolina, trained in Paris, and a member of the 1920s artistic movement known as the Harlem Renaissance, she died in 1995 in New Hope.

And, oh yes, that work of Selma Burke's art you possess? Well, if you possess a Roosevelt dime and look at the profile of FDR on it, you look upon her 1943 bas relief of the president.

Paul Licitra was a close friend and confidante of Dr. Burke. "I know that her spirit is around," he said. "I'll be laying on the couch watching television and I will feel someone walking. It's always around midnight."

A native of Syracuse, Paul was in the fashion world of New York City for 20 years. He "retired" to New Hope to enjoy the life as a "country squire." Although he resided on a farm for a while, his interest in the arts drew him in town and into his position as commissioner of the Arts Commission.

He also owned and operated the Towpath House for many years. During that time he and a talented staff actually reenacted the ghost stories of New Hope.

"I believe there are ghosts," he stated. "There are other entities other than our own physical selves. And, how they manifest is an interesting situation."

Adi-Kent Thomas-Jeffrey, whose earlier books included many ghost stories of New Hope and Bucks County, was a close friend of Paul's. "She called me 'Precious,'" he remembered with a fond grin. "She was a grand, elegant lady," he added.

It was she who discussed the "other side" often and intensely with Paul, and she who shaped his beliefs.

"It seems that you subconsciously are in tune to the same frequency as that particular aura, or ghost, and *you* actually manifest it and see the whole thing, rather than just a wave of air."

Paul still owns the properties at 18-20 Mechanic Street. And, he not only has heard all the stories about the ghosts there, but he has had some experiences of his own.

"One cold evening," he told us, "one of the waiters was stoking the fireplace. He was shaken for most of the evening. He didn't say anything, but I asked him what was the matter.

"He said that he was stoking the fireplace and saw someone standing close to him. He turned around and there was a woman in black, with a cane. He said she had gray hair and he asked her, 'Can I help you?'

"And then, he said, she just disappeared in front of him!"

With that, Paul invited Adi-Kent to investigate, and

she claimed that the woman in black was a former owner of the Towpath House who had fallen, broken her hip, and walked with a cane until the day she died.

"I have seen her myself," Paul said, "but not fully. I've seen a mist of her walking from one area to another.

"One time I was speaking to someone and I looked over their shoulder and I saw someone walking from the kitchen area into the restaurant. I said, 'I think I just saw a ghost!'"

On another occasion, he and a secretary were in the restaurant shortly after it had closed for the day.

"She heard the door, and she got up and asked 'Can I help you?' She heard nothing, so she went downstairs and heard the door to the bathroom open and close.

"So, she figured someone had come in to use the bathroom. She repeated her question.

"But nobody answered. Then, she yelled into the ladies room that if they didn't come out she'd call the police.

"Then, she decided she'd walk in. She did, and there was nobody in there."

The restaurant is on the lower level of the complex of buildings which is layered on the lay of the land as it slopes from the river up the hill to the cut of the canal. A tunnel extends from the building to the river and several mediums have said the tunnel, now inaccessible, is literally filled with spirit energy.

In one of the buildings which front Mechanic Street, several individuals have reported mysterious happenings.

"There was somebody living in a second floor apartment," Paul Licitra continued, "who told me they saw a globe of light–a filled globe–coming through the room. At first he thought it was a dream, but he knew it wasn't. He was actually seeing it."

This globe, or orb, was not the only entity that caught tenants unaware, according to Paul Licitra.

"My friend's mother was staying over in an apartment on the top floor. She told us about a dream she had about a man in a high hat and uniform who came down the steps and tried to sit on her bed.

"She said she tried to scream, but the scream wouldn't come out. She talked about it as if it was a nightmare.

"Well, it seems that the exact same thing had happened to quite a few people."

So, Paul Licitra owns haunted buildings in what is considered to be one of the most haunted towns in the country. What's more, he *lives* in a haunted house.

Is he at all concerned?

Not a whit.

"It's nice to know that there's another world, other than our own," he reasoned.

18-20 Mechanic Street, New Hope.

"DEVIL HARRY"

...and the Ghosts of the Pearl S. Buck House

The Pearl S. Buck House.

She was born in West Virginia, spent most of her childhood in China, went to college in Virginia, and returned to China as a young, married woman.

But it is Bucks County where the recipient of both the Nobel and Pulitzer prizes for literature spent nearly half of her life and in Bucks County where she established herself as one of America's finest writers and one of the world's champions of human rights.

Born Pearl Comfort Sydenstricker, she is etched in history as Pearl S. Buck.

Pearl was born to Southern Presbyterian missionary parents who took their five-month old baby back to Zhenziang in the autumn of 1892 after a brief reassignment in the United States.

During the Boxer Uprising of 1900, the Sydenstrickers returned to this country. Young Pearl graduated from Randolph-Macon Woman's College (1914), married agricultural economist John L. Buck (1917), and returned to Northern China as a newlywed.

During what was described as an unhappy, albeit 18-year marriage, the Bucks both taught at Nanking University, and had one natural and one adopted child.

Pearl S. Buck was published extensively throughout the 1920s and her experiences in China led to her classic *The Good Earth* in 1931.

That novel earned her the Pulitzer Prize and was adapted into a major motion picture. Following several more novels and works of non-fiction, she became the first American woman to win the Nobel Prize for Literature.

Having divorced John Buck, Pearl married publisher Richard Walsh in 1935. The couple settled at Green Hills Farm, adopted six more children, and worked together as tireless advocates of worldwide civil rights, Asian and American relations, the adoption of displaced interracial children, and the needs of the mentally retarded.

Most of her hundreds of books, articles, and short stories were written at her beloved Bucks County farm. All of her humanitarian work was conducted from that base. It was in Vermont where she passed away on March 6, 1973, but it is in a quiet grove on the 60-acre Green Hills Farm that Pearl Sydenstricker Buck rests in eternal peace.

Recognized as a prime example of Pennsylvania rural architecture, the ca. 1835 fieldstone home became a National Historic Landmark in 1980.

The ten rooms of the farmhouse reflect Pearl S. Buck's intercontinental and intercultural passions. Rice china is set on a Pembroke table. Chinese figures grace a stained glass window. Pennsylvania stoneware jugs anchor the hand-carved Chinese hardwood desk at which she wrote *The Good Earth*.

The grounds are beautifully landscaped and maintain the legendary owner's love of nature.

But, there are also very strong indications that the *super*natural is quite active at Green Hills Farm and in its centerpiece mansion.

"We know there is something in there," special events associate Trudy Gracin told us.

The "we" represents several individuals who tend or work at the property. The "something" represents one or more spirits that roam the property. The "there" is, more specifically, one particular room of the house, up for debate.

"It was the bedroom which was occupied by one of her adopted children," Ms. Gracin added.

Marty Nichols, the site's tour coordinator who often closes the home after its public operating hours, has also heard several stories of mysterious sounds–and, sometimes, sights.

"I heard that a housekeeper here, years ago, saw a woman in colonial dress walking through that bedroom," she said.

There was one other individual with very close connections to Green Hills Farm who heard the stories of ghostly activity.

"I have never seen our ghost," that individual is quoted as saying, "but our hired man insisted that 'Devil Harry' walks every Christmas Eve at midnight from the barn to the bridge and back again, and that anybody who knew what he looked like can see him plainly."

That individual who wrote those words was Pearl S. Buck.

She wrote of her Bucks County homestead–and of its spirits–in her autobiographical 1954 book *My Several Worlds*.

In that volume it was quite evident that Ms. Buck treasured the history, the heritage, the legends, and even the ghost of Green Hills Farm.

"It was even pleasant to discover a ghost belonging to our house," she wrote as an introduction to a fairly lengthy and detailed account of "Devil Harry" and other entities.

Then, in her crafty style, she melded the tales of her youth in China with the tales of her adulthood in her adopted Bucks County.

"China ghosts," she noted, "are nearly always women, the vapory souls of beautiful women, part fox, part fairy, who incarnate themselves again in living female bodies.

"Our ghost, however, is a Pennsylvania Dutchman, Old Harry, politely called, but usually Devil Harry."

This is a good time to interject the influence of a culture which has been all but obliterated by the gentrification and upscaling of much of Bucks County in recent decades.

While diverse influences have created a cosmopolitan demographic in the county, certain pockets of both the early Quaker and larger Pennsylvania German (erroneously but generally referred to as "Dutch," after "Deutsch," the native word for German) influences throughout Bucks.

Those pockets are deep in the legends and lore of the county.

Many of Bucks County's most prominent historical characters (i.e.: John Fries) were of German stock–Pennsylvania "Dutch." The German influence is still prevalent in many place names (i.e.: Trumbauersville). Noted Bucks Countians (i.e.: Henry Mercer, who studied Pennsylvania German "fraktur" art) have worked to preserve that influence.

And, ancient German traditions such as *broucha*, a form of faith-healing known colloquially as "powwowing" were carried out in the countryside throughout the county.

Pearl S. Buck wrote and spoke often about that rich Pennsylvania "Dutch" culture and seemed to hold it in high esteem.

As for "Devil Harry," his story is recalled by many insiders at Green Hills Farm.

Doris Brown, whose service as a docent there dates to the late 1970s, has heard all the stories but, in her words, "I'm not the sort who would go consciously to look for them (the ghosts)."

Ms. Brown's feelings for the property are strong.

She is related to the Moyer family from whom Pearl Buck purchased the farm.

Although Doris has never seen Devil Harry or any of the other spirits that roam the farm and farmhouse, she knows several folks who have. Several quite credible folks.

She knows where and when "Old Harry" can be found, and knows of the mysterious Mennonite woman who appears near the barn in springtime and lingers until the last leaves have fallen and the last blooms have faded.

Did, in fact, Pearl S. Buck see a ghost?

In *My Several Worlds*, she mentioned a woman whom she met but once along the lane which leads to the barn. Ms. Buck's description of her mode of dress matched that of a Mennonite. "When she came near," Buck wrote, "I saw that she was old and that she looked frightened. Her full round face, white and softly wrinkled, was unsmiling, and her dark eyes were like a child's in terror."

In the encounter, Pearl asked the stranger what she sought. The woman in black said she was born in the house and just came back to see what improvements Pearl had made and to see the "shrubbage."

After Ms. Buck invited her visitor to look around as long as she chose, the woman disappeared.

"I asked my neighbors about her," Buck wrote, "but

none knew who she could have been. Our hired man simply insisted that she was a ghost, too."

While that woman–real or surreal–was gentle, "Devil Harry" could stir up quite a fuss to all whose paths he crossed.

Still, Pearl S. Buck was unfazed. "The ghost has never molested us," she said. "Man, woman and children, we have lived peacefully and happily in the house."

•

AND, IN THE END...

...there is no end.

One fact became clear as we attempted to finalize our research and close our *Ghost Stories of Bucks County* project: It can never be finalized, never be closed.

As those who walked this pathway before us found out, and as those yet to tread this trail will discover, there is no end to the stories.

When one stack of notes, clippings, tapes, and pictures was whittled away to become the preceding chapters, another stack materialized as questions remained unanswered–and perhaps unanswerable.

Publication constraints prevented us from finding out more about some very intriguing old tales in this most intriguing old county.

Does the ghost of Congressman Caleb Taylor, a friend of Abraham Lincoln, still haunt the old Sunbury Farm land near Bristol?

Can there be any truth whatsoever that a lantern-holding ghost–said by some to be a former king of Spain–can be seen in a rowboat in the Delaware along the Bristol riverfront?

Is it true that if you sit in the "Witch's Chair" in a certain cemetery in Bristol you will be touched by a witch? Has anyone really ever picked up the notorious "Midnight Mary," who hitchhikes after dark on roads along the river? Does that Hessian soldier's ghost still prowl the basement of the Tate House at the George School near Newtown?

Is the old Community House, now law offices on N. Pennsylvania Ave. in Morrisville really haunted, as was reported in the late 1970s?

Why is so little remembered about the spiritualism hysteria in Doylestown in the early 1850s? Does anyone recall the stories of an active witch in Upper Black Eddy in the 1960s?

We could go on, and on, and on.

Unreturned phone calls, unresponsive inquiries, undocumentable incidents–all have left in their wakes questions to be answered some time, by some one in the future.

We hope you have enjoyed this collection of stories and have a new appreciation for the wealth of lore, the richness of legend, and the bounty of ghost stories in this most fascinating county.

• • •

ACKNOWLEDGMENTS

The researchers, author, and publisher are grateful to the following sources and resources who contributed to the compilation and completion of this book. We apologize for any omissions.

Newspapers, Magazines, Books, etc.

Bucks County *Courier-Times*, *The Intelligencer Record*, The *Daily Intelligencer*, Philadelphia *Inquirer*, Philadelphia *Bulletin*, Philadelphia *Record*, *The New York Times*, *Early Taverns of Bucks County* (William M. Rivinus, 1965) *Place Names in Bucks County Pennsylvania* (George MacReynolds, 1955), *Old Bucks County* magazine, *The Doylestown Patriot*, *Antiques & Auction News*, *Haunted Houses USA* (Dolores Riccio and Joan Bingham), *The Free Press*, Quakertown; *The Morning Call*, Allentown; A Collection of Papers, Vol. 1, by B.F. Fackenthal Jr.; *Albert Large: The Hermit Naturalist of Bucks County, Pa.* (William C. Armstrong), *Pennsylvania Illustrated*, *Bucks County Historical Society Journal, Bucks County Life, Annals of Philadelphia and Pennsylvania in the Olden Time* (John F. Watson, 1844), *Glimpses of Beautiful Bucks County* (Bucks County School Directors Assn., 1949), *Nouveau* magazine

Libraries, Historical Societies, Museums, etc.

Bucks County Historical Society, Spruance Library, Mercer Museum, Doylestown; Morrisville Free Library, Morrisville; Free Library of New Hope and Solebury, Friends of Bolton Mansion, Springfield Township Historical Society, Bucks County Community College, Newtown Historic Association, Historical Society of Pennsylvania

Individuals, Organizations

Monica Hartzel, Theresa Adams, Frank and Jane Hartzel, Philadelphia Ghost Hunters Alliance, Lew Gerew, Sharon Gerew, Bucks County Tourist Commission, Bucks County Conference & Visitors Bureau, Inc., Buckwampun Historical Society, Bucks County Department of Parks and Recreation, Pennsylvania Department of Conservation & Natural Resources, Bureau of State Parks, The Doylestown Business & Community Alliance, Bucks County Bed & Breakfast Association, New Hope Chamber of Commerce, Central Bucks Chamber of Commerce,

New Hope Arts Commission, Betty Riter

Miscellaneous

Alfred B. Patton, Inc., *Book Notes* TV show, http://theshadowlands.net, http://www.bucksnet.com, http://www.bucks32.com, http://www.visitbucks.com, http://phillyburbs.com,

Exeter House Books

Publishers of Quality Books on Legends, Folklore, History and Ghosts of the Mid-Atlantic States Since 1982

•

Available Titles

•

·Bucks County Ghost Stories
·Philadelphia Ghost Stories
·New York City Ghost Stories
·Ghost Stories of Pittsburgh and Allegheny County
·Pennsylvania Dutch Country Ghosts
·Pocono Ghosts, Legends & Lore, Book I
·Pocono Ghosts, Legends & Lore, Book II
·Ghost Stories of the Lehigh Valley
·Ghost Stories of the Delaware Coast
·Ghost Stories of Berks County, Book I
·Ghost Stories of Berks County, Book II
·Ghost Stories of Berks County, Book III
·Berks the Bizarre
·Cape May Ghost Stories, Book I
·Cape May Ghost Stories, Book II
·Legends of Long Beach Island
·Shipwrecks, Sea Stories & Legends of the Delaware Coast
·Shipwrecks & Legends 'round Cape May
·Shipwrecks Off Ocean City, New Jersey
·Shipwrecks Near Barnegat Inlet
·Great Train Wrecks of Eastern Pennsylvania
·The New York City Fire Patrol: An Illustrated History
·Joe's Boys: The Story of the Ferko String Band
·Tom Fox's Jersey Shore
·Ghost Stories of Berks County *(Audio Cassette read by the author)*
·Reading, Pa., Mirror to the Past *(Picture Book)*
·Cape May: Mirror to the Past *(Picture Book)*

•

ALL TITLES ARE AVAILABLE AT BOOK STORES AND THROUGH MAJOR INTERNET BOOKSELLERS

For More Information, write to Exeter House Books
PO Box 8134, Reading PA 19603